A Quiet Fortune

TERRIE DRAKE

Complete Collection: Books 1–4

Published by Brown Bag Books,
P.O. Box 1492, Glenwood Springs, CO 81602.

Layout by Nuria Moya.

Note: This publication contains the opinions and ideas of
its author. It is intended to provide helpful and informative
material on the subject matter concerned. It is sold with the
understanding that the author and publisher are not engaged
in rendering professional services in the book. If the reader
requires personal assistance or advice, a competent professional
should be consulted.

This book and its companion volume are available at special
quantity discounts for bulk purchases for sales promotions,
premiums, fund-raising, or educational use. For more
information, visit www.aquietfortune.com.

ISBN: 978-0-9965243-1-5

"The building of a Quiet Fortune should be as natural as breathing."

–Terrie Drake

Table of Contents

Introduction: Why Read These Little Books?...................6

BOOK ONE: A Powerful Force 9

Chapter 1: The Most Important Money Lesson...................10
Compound Interest Example One 11
Compound Interest Example Two 14
Yes, That Stinks. And No, That's Great! 17
The Kids: Let's Get Back to Them 18
Compound Interest Example Three 19
Tommy's Little Sister...................22

Chapter 2: How People Get to Their Very Own "Forever Fortunes"... 24
What Happened to Retirement? 27
Compound Interest Example Four 30
A Common Problem...................33

Chapter 3: How Do We Look at the Future? 34
Group One: Those "I Will" People Mean Business! 35
Group Two: Money Scaredy-Cats...................36
Group Three: Get Yourself a Plan, Stan 38
Are You Learning From Experience? 41

Chapter 4: How This Whole Thing Works...................44
What's So Interesting About Interest? 47
The Mom and Pop Plan Chart...................48
The Parameters of This Mom and Pop Plan 50
"The End of the Chart" Story...................53
Lessons Learned 54

Questions and Answers...................55

A Few Points Before Book One Ends...................58

What's Coming Next...................60

BOOK TWO: Learn, Invest, Teach 63

Chapter 1: The Basics of Investing...................................64
How to Get Started: If Your Employer Will Help 67
What if You're On Your Own? 69
Step One: Call Your Bank or Credit Union........................70
Step Two: Make Regular Deposits 71
Step Three: Mutual Funds – Get one 72
Why Mutual Funds? 73
Ways to Learn About Mutual Funds.................................75
Some Terms You'll Learn...77
What the Heck is a Prospectus?.......................................79
Are You Ready? Just Do It!...80
Finally, Make that Mutual Fund an IRA 81
Want to Learn With Less Effort? 82
Kind of Advisors...83
That Old Savings Account..85
What if the Market Tanks? 86

Chapter 2: Need an Incentive? Step Back Five Years.............88
As Ordinary as Breathing...91

Chapter 3: Teach the Kids About Their Own Quiet Fortunes........92
Influence...94
The Quiet Fortune Lesson..95
Why Don't We Save?..96
Never Too Old? Never Too Young! 98
When Your Child is Small 100
More Than One Account 101
When Your Child Gets Older 102
A Sense of Control..103
Good Decision? Bad Decision?.......................................107
Make-Your-Own Bank Night...108
About the Giving Box 109
Should My Child Get an Allowance? 113
That Savings Account at the Bank...................................116

Chapter 4: Boy, Can That Kid Add! 118

What Have You Accomplished So Far? 119

When Your Child is Eight Years Old 121

A Happy Tenth Birthday Present 122

This One's Forever 124

A Little Later 125

Twelve: A Great Age to Be 126

The Best Money Lesson Ever 131

Now, Really: Why Do This the Long Way? 139

This is How We Remember Stuff! 140

BOOK THREE: It's So E.A.S.Y. For Young People 143

Chapter 1: A Real Fortune is Ahead 144

To One Smart Kid: You 146

A Tale of Two Savers 147

The Growth of Ana's and Shawn's Savings Chart 148

The Growth of Ana's and Shawn's Savings 150

The Guy With $42 151

Do Most Teens Save and Invest? 152

You're Smarter Than That 155

It's E.A.S.Y.: The Power of Ten Bucks 156

What Should You Know to Build a Quiet Fortune? 161

Chapter 2: Five Little Ideas that can Make a Big Difference 162

Money Concept One 163

Apples to Apples 165

Why You Absolutely Need to Know This 167

How to Get Compound Interest Working for you Today 168

Money Concept Two 170

Money Concept Three 172

Money Concept Four 175

Money Concept Five 177

So There You Have It: Five Things You Need to Know 180

Chapter 3: Beyond the Math – Jobs, College, Out on Your Own ... 182

So, How Do You "Get" Money? 183

Saving Some of this New Money 185

A Few Ideas to Help You Spend Less 186

College: Will This Kill Your Investment Fund? 187

About Those Credit Card Offers 189

College and Your Forever Fortune Money 191

What One Smart Man Said 192

Debt: Go Into or Stay Out Of? 193

When You're Out of College and On Your Own 195

How Much Better for You! 197

Some Tips from "The Experts" 200

BOOK 4: The VIPs: Very Important Parents and Grands 203

To All You Very Important People, Parents and Grands 204

Personal Choices 206

Where to Start 207

One Simple Concept, One Simple Habit 209

What Have We Covered? 210

What Big Income? 212

A Note for You Grandparents 214

Wisdom of Wealth 216

Appendix 218

Works Cited 232

INTRODUCTION

Why Read These Little Books?

Mark's a regular guy with a regular job. By the time he's 62 he will have well over half a million dollars. His best friend Robbie will have acquired almost nothing.

When she's 65 Ana will own an investment portfolio of approximately a million dollars. Shawn, who graduated from college the same year, will end up with less than half that.

At retirement Tommy's sister will have almost $1,190,000. She will have spent $66,000 to get to that amount. Her cousins, despite doing almost the same thing she did, will not come close to her level of wealth.

What did Mark, Ana, and Tommy's sister do that will make such a difference in their lifetime prosperity? Very little, actually. They didn't risk much. They weren't incredibly money-savvy. They didn't start with a bundle of money or inherit a fortune.

They all did one thing, though, that changed the course of their lives. They got advice from someone – a parent, a relative, or a teacher – and followed it. They took a couple of steps that were profoundly important even though they seemed trivial at the time.

Mark, Ana, and Tommy's sister were both fortunate and smart: they got the advice that would make them wealthy and they paid attention to it.

Countless young people, hearing the same thoughts from someone they trust, would benefit in ways we can't even begin to imagine.

This Book Shares The Secret

Plenty of plans exist for building wealth, of course. People might become entrepreneurs with the hope of becoming rich. If they love the business and are willing to work hard their dreams may come true. Some people hear about moneymaking schemes and work at them. Other people might buy lottery tickets with the same dream of big bucks in mind.

Some of us risk everything; others resign ourselves to lives of financial worry.

The ideas in these little books are less risky and much easier than schemes and dreams. They are real, honest, surprisingly simple. You could call them the "lazy" way to financial security.

These concepts are uniquely powerful for young people, not necessarily for those of us who are already a lot older: time is the most important factor. Our kids need our guidance to get to the realization that they can build considerable wealth.

You – the parents, grandparents, friends, and teachers of children and young adults – can pass these hints on. Your knowledge and your advice will make all the difference in the world to the young people you care about.

Book One
A Powerful Force

Chapter One:

The Most Important Money Lesson

For generations a very simple way has existed for
us to put ourselves on a sound financial footing.
In plain language this book tells the story of how we,
as parents and grandparents, can look at money.
We can easily teach our children about it, and our
kids can grow wealth steadily.

Don't look for miracles or get-rich-quick schemes here.

No, that's not right, look for one big miracle:
it's known as compound interest. Albert Einstein is credited
for calling compound interest "The Most Powerful Force in
the Universe." Whether he actually said that or not has been
challenged, but Einstein was more than impressed with its
potential. We should be too. So let's not waste any time.
This is the basis of wealth building for our children.

Compound Interest Example One

Wow! A Whole DOLLAR?

What is Compound Interest? It's the money we make when we invest some of our money, and then keep investing the original principal as well as the interest we just earned. Here's an example:

During the first year of an investment of $100 we would make ten dollars in interest if we put our money in something that returns ten percent. So after one year we have $110. The compounding part comes the next year when our invested amount is now $110. That second year we will make:

> $110
> x   .10 (10%)
> $ 11 = Look at that: eleven dollars!

We'll make one dollar more than we did the first year because:

- We have once again made ten dollars on our original investment, but now:

- We have also made an extra dollar. We kept our interest in the account and earned interest on the interest,

- Not just on the original $100.

Our interest has compounded.

You may be thinking, "Big deal: a whole dollar more. Do you seriously think it's time to celebrate?"

Actually, it is a big deal. Certainly not this year, or the next. But imagine that our $100 plus ten percent grew every single year for a long time. If we were young enough when we first put that $100 in an investment, say ten years old, we'd have $11,739.09 by the time we turned sixty.

Now that's a big deal. We started with $100 at the age of ten. We added nothing to our original $100. That little amount will turn into almost $12,000 along about retirement time. That's the magic of compound interest.

There has to be a catch, right?

Actually, there are two.

The first is the way I'm going to use one word: "interest." It usually refers to guaranteed investments in which you are paid for loaning your money to someone. We get that kind of interest if we invest in certificates of deposit, savings accounts, or money market accounts. But in today's world that kind of investment will not earn anywhere near enough to make a difference in the future. Those guaranteed investments are long gone.

We can still make money, though, in other types of investments while we apply the idea of compound interest. In these books I'll use the word "interest" to refer to the money we earn in investments that may not be guaranteed, but that have proven to be solid for many decades.

The second and most important catch seems to be that the vast majority of us really don't catch on to the idea of money compounding over time. We may learn something about it in school but we don't really get a chance to put it into practice for our own benefit. Or we are too old to use its power.

The key, as I hinted at, is Time. With a capital "T."

It's hard to make compounding interest work easily for us when we get older. We simply don't have enough time. We can't invest just a little bit of money, yet end up wealthy, if we are in our 40s or 50s before we start to think seriously about our futures. By that age we have to go to Plan B or C.

> **You can't get rich quick. You only get rich slowly, over a lifetime of effort. Fantasizing about being rich does not take you there.**
>
> – Dr. Phil DeMuth[1]

But Plan A, using the power of Compounding Interest, is simple and attainable, especially if we don't have large sums of money coming in.

That's why this concept, although helpful for all of us, is mostly for the kids. They do have time. And we parents and grandparents can help them in very easy ways to start a future that will be filled with security.

Let me give you another example of this miracle of compounding interest. But first, here's a tip:

Sometimes we look at lists of numbers and it all seems like a blur. That's not a good way to learn. The examples in this book of the power of compound interest are not just charts, they are stories of people like you and me.

I wish many of us had heard these stories years ago. Somehow, even though we actually knew that we should be saving, many of us never knew how much easier it would be if we had just started earlier.

Einstein was right about that "most powerful force" thing.

Compound Interest Example Two

Todd's Woulda, Coulda, Shouldas

Todd is 45 years old. He has saved enough money to put $10,000 away for retirement, and he's feeling pretty good about it. He will put the money into a mutual fund (more about these simple investment vehicles in a later book) and thinks he can earn eight percent on average. He knows that during some years he will lose money, but in other years he might make 20 percent or more, so he feels fairly confident about the average over time.

One day Todd decides to figure out how much his $10,000 will grow to by the time he is 65. A simple calculation shows:

$10,000
x _____.08 (8%)
$ 800 (Interest he will earn in 1 year)

Plus the original $10,000 gives him a total of:
    $10,800

He'll have this at the end of a year. Great!

But now Todd knows the figuring gets more complicated because the interest amount will change every year as his money compounds. He goes to the Internet and searches for "financial calculators." (Bankrate.com is a good site, quoted by many financial writers.) He clicks on a fairly straightforward "interest savings" calculator.

There he enters:
    $10,000   Initial investment
        0   Added monthly *(he doesn't have more)*
        8%   Interest, compounded monthly
        20   Years until his retirement

Within a split second Todd finds out that his $10,000 should become $49,268 by the time he retires. Great! In 20 years (which actually seems fairly short, now that he's looking at his "golden years") he will have made more than $39,000, just by sticking some money into an investment today. Hmm ... sounds good.

By now Todd is interested. Having almost $50,000 will be great. But in truth it's not even close to enough cash to retire comfortably on and Todd is well aware of that. With his job's retirement account and Social Security so uncertain, who knows what will happen in 20 years?

Still on the financial calculator website, Todd is curious about how much money he might have if he had squirreled $10,000 away ten years earlier. So this time he gives the calculator 30 years for his $10,000 to grow.

Hmm ... could that be right? It shows a total of $109,357! That's way more than twice what his money will be worth in 20 years – and by adding on only half that amount of time.

Not quite believing it, Todd again checks his result. Yes. It's over $109,000 – from a start of $10,000 and not having added a penny more. All he needed to do was keep it invested for a longer time. Todd looks at the numbers again, giving his original investment more and more time to grow. Here's what Todd finds out:

If Todd Started at Age:	And His Money Grew at 8% for ____ Years:	By Age 65 He Would Have:
45	20	$49,268
35	30	$109,357
25	40	$242,734
15	50	$538,782

That's amazing: if by some miracle Todd had been given $10,000 when he was 15 years old and had just stuck it someplace to get eight percent interest and forgotten about it, by the time he was ready to quit work he would have over half a million dollars! Unbelievable.

... Right. Well, so much for pretending. There's no way anyone in his family would have been able to give him $10,000 at any time in his life, especially not when he was 15 years old.

But heck, a person can dream, can't he? Might as well see what would have happened if that Magical-Great-Uncle-Make-Believe had left him $10,000 when he was only ten years old.

Let's see: $10,000 to begin, with:
              55 years to invest, earning:
              8% interest on average
Would be: **$802,702**

Over $800,000! That's a huge improvement over the $49,000 Todd realistically hopes to get.

Life sometimes stinks, doesn't it?

Yes, That Stinks. And No, That's Great!

It's hard to face the reality of not having enough money. It means worry and fret at the very least. All is not lost for Todd, though. After all, he is 20 years away from quitting work. There is still time to get a small second job, one that will allow him to stash some serious money into investments and let him worry less about retirement even though he will have to work more, at least for a few years.

Todd should start right away by talking to a financial advisor, someone he trusts to give him solid advice and lead him through decisions for the next few years. Or Todd could begin by reading about how to plan for retirement.

But while he is getting his own future in order Todd should, right this very minute, begin to help his children discover this truth much earlier than he did.

If we begin saving and investing early we can eventually enjoy a life of genuine financial freedom.

The Kids:
Let's Get Back to Them

Even though we ourselves may have to take a different path to become financially secure, our children are perfectly placed to take advantage of the concepts in these books.

Time and the magic of compounding interest are the keys.

I just gave you an example of how an investment of $10,000 early on can make all the difference.

But in reality most people would find it difficult if not impossible to give each of their children $10,000 when they turn ten. Or at any age, for that matter. Most young parents can barely scrape by during those early family years and it takes a while for them to get on solid footing. Is this idea of compounding interest all just a big dream, then?

No. It absolutely holds true. And even though a rich relative might be a great solution to our money needs, it's only one way to be sure our children are secure.

There's another way to accumulate a first fortune. For most of us, it's much more realistic and it teaches the kids along the way: it's through small sums added slowly.

Compound Interest Example Three

Four – No, Make that Five – Cousins

Robert, Mark, Jane and Tommy are cousins. They certainly don't have anyone to give them $10,000, but at a family reunion they all agree that they will start putting their own money away for the future. They have all had jobs since high school and each can stash the same amount every month: $100. That's $1,200 per year that each cousin has decided to put away for a long, long time.

These cousins are smart. They know they will most likely work until they are 65, and that looks like forever away. In fact, it's laughable for them to even imagine being that old. To quote one cousin, "I'd rather be dead than 60!" But they have seen their parents worry about money and they want to avoid going through the same stress.

The facts are all the same:

- Each will probably work until age 65,

- Each plans to put away $100 per month,

- The stock market fund they use is identical, and

- That fund will probably earn an average of eight percent each year.

Only one thing is different – their ages:

- **Robert** is 25,

- **Mark** is 35,

- **Jane** is 45, and

- **Tommy** (whose brother Robert has "conned" him into investing) is 15 years old.

How much will each of the cousins have by the time they retire at 65?

Cousin (Age)	Years to Invest	Total Invested	Total by Age 65	Will Have Made a Profit of:
Jane (45)	20	$24,000	**$58,907**	$34,907
Mark (35)	30	$36,000	**$149,047**	$113,047
Robert (25)	40	$48,000	**$349,125**	$301,125
Tommy (15)	50	$60,000	**$793,227**	$733,227

Now look at Tommy's numbers. Here are the facts:

- He starts very young.

- He has odd jobs, allowances, and some birthday money.

- He somehow collects $100 each month to stash away.

- Even in college, he works extra hours to keep that $100 per month payment going.

- All the time he works in his career, marries, has a family, and goes through life he somehow keeps that $100 each month going into investments.

- Even when he gets promotions he feels okay moving just $100 into his "Forever Fortune," as he calls it.

- Over the years he will have invested a total of $60,000.

Tommy ends up with **$793,227**. He has made a profit of over $733,000.

Tommy will make almost $700,000 more than Jane did, and it will cost him only $36,000 more than she will have invested.

As they save for the future, Tommy and his wife will learn to trust themselves as to what their family needs right away and what might have to be put on the list to buy later. But they will always make sure that they pay themselves first by moving some money into their "Forever Fortune" account each month. And guess what? Tommy will retire with more money than lots of people in his town who had made much more over their careers.

The "magic," of course, is that Tommy had learned about compounding interest from his brother and cousins. They will do well, but because he was so much younger Tommy will have almost three-quarters of a million more than his oldest cousin Jane has by retirement time, and more than double what his brother Robert (who is only ten years older) makes.

▌ Tommy's Little Sister

> ## Money is better than poverty, If only for financial reasons.
>
> – Woody Allen

To really make a point, let's take this one step further. Let's imagine that Tommy's little sister, who is ten, starts a savings account. She does the same thing the four cousins have done. Of course, because she's so young she can't achieve a goal of saving $100 per month for quite a few years. But she has set that goal and does save some of her birthday and babysitting money. Later on she puts $200 in every month until she catches up to her goal. It's hard but she's had some good role models who check on her progress from time to time.

This is what Tommy's younger sister will have at the end of her working career:

She will have invested:	$66,000 *(only $6,000 more than Tommy)*
For a total of:	55 years *(now that's a long time)*
And will end up with:	$1,189,133
That's a profit of:	**$1,123,133**

From an investment of $66,000 over her lifetime, this young person will have well over a million dollars to retire on, not to mention any company 401(k)s or Social Security she will have accumulated. That amount, even with inflation factored in, will let her live on the interest and never touch the principal. Although she may not ever work at a really high-paying job, she'll be comfortable, secure, and able to enjoy retirement. And it's all because of starting early with a goal that can be achieved each month.

It's time to move those numbers into your own children's lives. It is completely possible for your children to build a quiet fortune for their retirement years.

They don't have to:

- Live in poverty now,
- Inherit a bundle of money from you, or
- Rob a bank.

What they need to do is:

- **Start early,**
- **Save some of their money and invest it, and**
- **Make saving a natural part of their lives.**

You can help. Helping your child to do these things takes some thinking. It's not hard though; in fact, the steps are simple.

This all-important concept, The Magic of Compounding Interest, can become a part of your indisputable knowledge about the world. There is plenty of time for you to teach your kids about saving and investing. The important thing now is that you need to KNOW your children can be more than okay financially if they just do a few things early enough.

I'll show you some very basic steps to wise investing in the next chapters and in Book Two. It's all a natural progression and takes very little time to teach your children.

A final word: If you're not as secure financially as you would like to be, you're in big company. The vast majority – 92 percent – of working households age 25-64 has retirement account balances that do not meet minimum savings benchmarks.[2] Your own thoughts about financial security and wise money dealings will grow as you pass your knowledge on to your children. Becoming financially independent can become a family affair.

It doesn't have to be just a rich man's world.

Chapter Two:

How People Get to Their Very Own "Forever Fortunes"

You have just seen three examples of the power of compounding interest.

- The first gave you the basic idea using $100.

- In example two you watched while Todd realized what his $10,000 could have turned into.

- The last showed five cousins who saved the same amount monthly but for different lengths of time.

The big idea here, and the big idea for building a Forever Fortune, is to know that interest compounded can become a force all its own. It's not just the foundation; it can become the walls, the roof, and the entire fortune itself, given enough time.

We'll look next at a plausible way for your child to begin to build that Forever Fortune without first collecting $10,000 or having to begin at a ridiculously young age.

But before we do that we should know that this plan for building wealth is not just a fun idea we can toss around. It's an absolute necessity. Today in the United States we're facing a crisis that will affect our children even more than it's affecting us.

The crisis is retirement – or, rather, the lack of a retirement.

Today far too many 60- and 70-somethings are still on their feet all day, still working despite getting to the age when work is harder to find and harder to do. It's probably not just because they all love getting up in the morning and hustling off to fairly low paying jobs. It's often because they have to.

Maybe they had medical bills they couldn't pay. Maybe a divorce or spouse's death took their savings. Maybe their previous jobs did not have retirement benefits.

Maybe, maybe, maybe. The fact is, a crisis is looking us straight in the eye and it's frightening. By far, most of us don't have enough money saved and our retirement plans have vanished or dried up or were legislated into completely different creatures. And far too many of us are stuck.

The statistics – and there are plenty of them – are alarming. Here are just two:

1. Advisors are telling us that we should have at least seven times our yearly incomes saved as we near retirement. As recently as only a few years ago, though, **over seventy-five million Americans had not put even one penny toward their retirement.**[3]

2. In August, 2014 CBS Evening News reported that
    36% of Americans 65 years old had still not saved a thing.

The facts about our retirement savings are more than just worrisome, they are forcing many of us to panic. And we should be concerned. The average retirement account in the U.S. for people nearing their mid-60s is only about $40,000.

> *We shall scrimp and save!*
> *Will you still need me,*
> *Will you still feed me,*
> *When I'm 64?*
>
> – The Beatles

What Happened to Retirement?

Once upon a time in America, from the 1950s to the early 1980s, huge numbers of workers were fairly well set for their later years. They typically worked for one company most of their careers, had money deducted for Social Security and/or another retirement plan and retired with what was called a Defined Benefit pension. Defined benefit was just that: the benefits they would get were defined – or spelled out – even before retirement so workers knew what they could count on.

Those plans were good for workers, if not so much for the employers. Not only did retirees know how much they would get, they also knew they would receive that amount every single month of their lives. And their spouses would get a benefit after they died: guaranteed.

Defined benefit (DB) plans had other advantages:

> In traditional DB plans, employers bear the investment risk and primary funding responsibility, [and] assets are usually managed by professionals ... Because they are pooled, defined benefit pensions provide significantly higher retirement income than defined contribution plans [where you know what you'll need to contribute, but not what you will receive in retirement or for how many years; that will depend upon the stock market].[4]

With the assurance that a certain amount of money would always be coming in, workers did not have to be obsessively concerned about saving for retirement. They saved, yes, but the pressure was less: they did not need to have an enormous amount stashed away. After all, they could not outlive their monthly allotment.

So what happened? Basically, companies replaced defined benefit plans with others that were fiscally more beneficial to them. Some dropped their retirement plans altogether. By 1988 only 54 percent of employers sponsored a retirement plan.[5] This was somewhat easier to do than you might think because ten years before that a federal law had been passed creating 401(k) plans.

55% of current workers don't have any employment-based savings at all.[6]

Although 401(k)s had a few advantages over the older DB plans (a worker could carry them from job to job, for example) they were never meant to replace defined benefit plans. But by 1988 many companies were on the way to making the worker research and fund his or her own retirement.

Today only the workers that are closest to retirement still have defined benefit plans, and only about 60 percent of them at that. In addition, by 2011 only 52 percent of private sector employees age 25-64 had access to any retirement plan on the job – the lowest rate since 1979.

Today, if they have a plan at all, most workers are exposed to "a host of risks that they are ill-equipped to bear as individuals: inadequate contributions, poor investment choices, financial market volatility, and outliving their retirement savings."[7]

Times have changed, and workers are suddenly realizing that their after-work years are sadly underfunded.

I could quote statistic after worrisome statistic. I won't, but just to hint at the severity of the problem I'll tell you that:

- Among households approaching retirement, the median retirement account balance was only $12,000 by 2010. According to BlackRock it's higher than that by now, but not high enough: it should be from 7-11 times the household's annual income. That's from a low of $210,000 to over $1,000,000.

- In one report only 15 percent of employees are projected to have sufficient income at age 65, and

- About 44 percent of Baby Boomers and GenXers are at risk of not having enough income to meet even basic expenses in retirement.[8]

Help is out there for soon-to-be-retirees. We can start to learn as soon as we open books, open our awareness, open our thoughts to possible solutions. The situation is so widespread that we can find hundreds of books and thousands of financial advisors who can suggest a path to take. We may not reach retirement with a massive portfolio but we can make some decisions that will make life better later on.

In the meantime, what about our kids? Predictions for their future well-being are becoming more worrisome even than ours as the gap between the "haves" and the "have-nots" in this country continues to widen. Particularly if we ourselves are not wealthy our children absolutely must learn some proven ways to ensure their own financial stability. If we give them the right advice and a little bit of help their future prosperity will be far more likely.

I'm going to show you a way to help your kids not only avoid this calamity but actually end up with enough money in retirement to travel, enjoy life, and continue to prosper. The first three examples of compound interest gave you the basic idea. The story that's coming up, "Two Good Buddies," can make the idea attainable.

> *About half of Americans are in danger of not fully covering their basic living expenses in retirement, like housing, health care, and food.*
>
> *– John Sweeney, Exec. VP for Fidelity Investments[9]*

Compound Interest
Example Four
Two Good Buddies

Mark and Robbie had been best friends since they were little kids. They lived next door to each other, played trucks in the dirt pile between their houses, walked to school using the same shortcuts, did everything together.

As many friends do, though, Mark and Robbie grew apart as they got older. First there were girlfriends, then college and families. They would see each other at Christmas when they headed back to the old neighborhood but that was about all. Within time their class reunions helped them keep in touch. Those holidays and reunions always gave them a chance to visit for hours and they would part knowing that their friendship was a lasting one.

An interesting thing began to take place as the years came and went. Rob and Mark would talk about almost everything: their old school days, their jobs, kids, and parents. As they got older they would share information about which cars got the best mileage or how to save on insurance. But they never talked seriously about money. Our personal finances are one of the most forbidden subjects in our society, so it was natural that neither of them brought it up. Too bad.

You see, all the while Mark and Rob were creating their lives, Mark had been doing one thing that Rob hadn't: he had been creating a future.

It was almost an indiscernible difference. Both of them had worked for similar salaries through the years and made about an average income for their area. Generally their lives were fine, but neither felt as though they wasted money. Rob kept to a fairly tight budget but Mark didn't. There was one thing that Mark had done, however, that would bring a secure retirement to him with ease.

Mark had started investing when he was 18 years old.

As soon as Mark had graduated from high school he decided to put most of his graduation money to work. He talked to his money-savvy Aunt Maggie, got her advice, and started a mutual fund account. Every year from that year forward Mark stuck $2,000 into that account, switching it occasionally if other investments looked more sensible.

Those first few years of investing had been really tough; after all, $2,000 would have paid for books in college as well as more than a few party nights. But Mark was determined. He had seen some numbers in a high school economics class that made him think:

$2,000 a year invested at 7% for 42 years would grow to: $544,774

and that same $2,000 invested at 8% would total: $743,661

Mark figured that he would be putting aside a total of $84,000 if he invested this way, but that he would end up with hundreds of thousands more by the time he was 62. Not bad.

So with that little bit of information Mark decided to do whatever it would take. Even though he knew his money would not go as far in 42 years as it did then, he still loved the idea of being at least a "half millionaire" and maybe a real full-blown millionaire – just by saving.

Robbie had heard those same numbers in school. But retirement was a LIFETIME away. Heck, he'd be making a million a year by that time, he guessed. Why worry now?

It wasn't until Robbie was almost 50 that he thought about his "million-a-year" dream and woke up to the fact that all he had for retirement income was Social Security and a small matching 401(k) from the company. That would not do much toward making his life comfortable. In fact, he worried that it might not even buy necessities.

At their next visit Robbie asked Mark if he had thought about retirement. When Mark said confidently that he should be set to retire at 62, Rob was amazed to think that his best childhood friend had been thinking about it for years already.

"No," Mark replied. "I really don't think about it much at all. My saving and investing is so automatic that I just know it's happening. I quit missing that $2,000 by the time I was 24. I just didn't have it … it was mine to keep, not to pay bills with or to spend. I just took that old advice to pay myself first."

Impressed, Robbie went home to do a bit of calculating himself. Let's see, he wanted $500,000 to retire on also. But he decided he'd better plan on retiring a few years after Mark since he hadn't started saving yet … maybe he would retire at 65. He went to a personal finances website to calculate how much he would need to invest yearly if he made an initial deposit of $2,000 and earned about seven percent.

To start at age 50 and retire at 65 meant he would be investing for 15 years.

His goal was	$500,000
He would begin with	$2,000
And should make	7%
Compounded	monthly

Robbie hit the "Calculate" button:

That means he should plan to invest	**$1,559.50 per month**
Which equals	**$51.27 each day**
or	**$358.90 weekly**

What!? Why, that meant he would have to tuck away:

$18,714 per year!

Stunned, Robbie sat at his desk and wondered how he had put this off for so long. Here was his best buddy saving a mere $2,000 a year and he would have to save almost that every month for the next 15 years. How could this have happened?

▌A Common Problem

The story about Robbie's wake-up moment is more common than we might want to admit. In January 2013 the CBS Morning Show announced that only 42 percent of adults have crunched the numbers to know what they will need in retirement. A few other studies cite slightly higher numbers, but even their statistics are disturbing.

To add to the bad news, we all know that Social Security has been under scrutiny for years as an unsustainable entitlement but if it is still around it will only replace about 20 percent of our incomes.[10]

> Financially responsible and successful people don't build their wealth by accident – or overnight. Becoming rich takes serious willpower and long-term vision. You have to be able to keep your eye on the prize of financial freedom.
>
> – MarketWatch

Still, many of us hide our heads to a scary reality: a time will come when we want to stop working, or when we simply have to quit. If we have been thinking like Mark all along we can enjoy those golden years with some actual gold and a feeling of security and excitement. But if, like Rob, we ignored both reality and the incredibly positive phenomenon of compound interest, we'll probably panic.

Even though they were best friends Robbie and Mark had been looking at money in totally different ways.

Chapter Three:

How Do We Look at the Future?

There's a good chance that you and your friends might be miles apart in how you handle your finances too. Just knowing we have different views can help us realize that we might want to expand our own thoughts. Then we can teach our kids a few good ways to look at the future.

Generally, you can clump people into one of three different "money attitude" groups. They are:

- "I Will, I Will, I Will!" People

- "Money is Downright Frightening" Folks

- The "I Have a Plan" Gang

Group One
Those "I Will" People Mean Business!

I Will, I Will, I Will! people are absolutely determined to become financially comfortable. Many of them just know that they will work hard and succeed monetarily. They often start their own business at a young age, says Warren Buffett. They work long hours for many years and learn as much as possible about their area of expertise as well as about finances.

A person in this group may make novice mistakes along the way but is determined to continue until success is reached. He or she may define success using financial terms but usually gains a great deal of personal satisfaction from the work itself.

"I Will" people save as much money as possible, both to feed back into the business and to meet their goals of being well off financially. They may not need basic advice about how to save or invest money, but might want ideas about how their children can learn good money habits; the worries of the wealthy may be more centered on how to keep their children grounded in the world.

Group Two
Money Scaredy-Cats

The Money is Downright Frightening folks actually consist of three somewhat diverse, but all negative, attitudes:

DON'T LOOK NOW!

Don't Look Now! people are very much like the Robbie in our story. They use the Ostrich Method of dealing with finances. That is, they stick their heads in the sand and never think of their futures.

At first they don't look at the future because it's so very far away; then they don't look later on because it's too scary. They often work hard, live well and provide for their families, but they may go into credit card debt and simply put off the day that they will have to face some harsh realities.

Like all of the groups, Don't Look Now folks have been around forever. Remember Aesop's Fables and the story of the Grasshopper and the Ants? The grasshopper danced and fiddled the summer away while the ants worked to have plenty of grain stored for the coming winter. It was only when starvation looked him in the eye that the grasshopper realized the mistake he had made.

Many of us are Don't Look Now people. But you're not, I know it. If you were, you would not be reading this. No matter what you've thought in the past, you will have a plan, and one part of your plan will include helping your children learn to save. It's not only possible; it's actually exciting.

GOSH, I'LL TRY, BUT ...

This Money is Downright Frighting group are the men and women who start out by announcing that they'll get their finances in order but in the deep recesses of their minds they have already failed. As with a few other attempts they may have made to improve their lives, the Gosh, I'll Trys ... probably don't think they can succeed. They'll save for a bit but lose sight of the rewards and simply quit.

If you might be a Gosh, I'll Try, But ... person, KEEP READING! I'm convinced that many of us in this category just plain don't understand the amazing gains our children and we ourselves can make as money grows. That realization alone can move us into a more active, positive attitude. Money won't be frightening to this group if they just know about the pot of gold and all the possibilities that await them.

THE MISERS

The most troubling of the Money is Frightening group are The Misers. Misers think they're being frugal by holding tight to every penny, never giving any away or even allowing themselves to enjoy the occasional fling. But they, too, harbor the thought that money is something restricted, something to be frightened of.

To Misers, letting go of a portion of their wealth is like cutting another strand of the rope they're hanging onto while they dangle over their very own financial cliff. They do not believe that caring and sharing, using (and sometimes losing) money are important parts of life. Misers can make those around them miserable as they count, then stash, every dollar.

You might think that it would be okay to be something of a miser if you need to save. But it's not really: hoarding money is as debilitating as hoarding newspapers and old milk cartons.

If you start to save gently when you're relatively young, though, you can just put away a certain amount automatically. Then you can use all the rest of your paycheck to pay bills, put some aside for mid-term goals, and occasionally splurge with wild abandon. You'll still be on track and you'll feel good about your financial life, having fun along the way.

Group Three
Get Yourself a Plan, Stan

Finally, we have the I Have a Plan gang. These people have looked at the future and know it's possible to have an income stream even after they have quit working. They know this because they actually do have a feasible plan. They are the people who don't necessarily want to devote most of their time and effort just to making money, but who want to know they'll still be okay.

> Among the 'rules for creating wealth' are: First of all, <u>decide</u> to be wealthy.
>
> –Reynolds & Bexton[11]

Plenty of varieties of "Plans" exist. If you're wanting to get one for yourself but don't know how, you might want to talk to a financial advisor to get started. But when it comes to your children's needs, let's keep it simple. Basically, a child's financial future can be well established through one of these three plans:

RICH UNCLE PLAN
This is definitely the simplest plan of all. It doesn't involve doing a darned thing, as Ramona found out. She was just a little girl when her grandfather died and left her parents some money. They knew that a portion of their inheritance put away for Ramona right then (not to be touched until she was much older) would grow impressively. So they set aside $10,000 just for her. Neither Ramona nor her parents ever put another dollar into her account, but by the time Ramona was 60 years old and ready to retire, that account had grown at an average of seven percent yearly and had reached $442,000. By then it was earning $25,000 each year in interest. That interest, combined with Social Security and a solid 401(k) plan she had set up at work, would allow her to leave work without worrying. Talk about a windfall! With a plan like this you can help assure financial security for your child without much effort … provided you have a "rich uncle"-type relative tucked away somewhere. Hmm … that may be one small problem.

HIGH SCHOOL ECONOMICS PLAN

In the story about Robbie and Mark, while Robbie was a Don't Look Now! kind of guy, Mark adopted the High School Economics Plan. He had paid attention to the lessons he had gotten about compounding interest. As soon as he could, he started saving and investing the same dollar amount each and every year. His parents did not help him but because he had begun investing at the age of 18 he was set. And the interesting thing was, as soon as he had set up automatic transfers through his bank to his investment account ($167 each month for his working life) he rarely felt the pinch of saving.

High School Economics Plan people rapidly realize that their contributions to a separate investment account allow them to "Pay Themselves" rather than paying out money to everyone else. It feels good.

MOM AND POP PLAN

Mark's method might be the best. But we never really know if our children will be able to gather $2,000 in their late teens, then add that same amount yearly during the high cost days of college, marriage, new house and young children. But we as parents often find it hard to come up with a lump sum for our sons and daughters to invest; nor do we necessarily want to.

That's when the Mom and Pop Plan works. We start early – as early as possible – and put a very small amount aside for our children each year until they reach working age. They will have accrued around $10,000 by that time. Meantime, we teach them a little bit about how and why to save. When they pick up the responsibility they can continue with small amounts because they have the time factor of compounding interest on their side. That sudden panicky realization later in life of not having enough money won't happen.

This Mom and Pop Plan will work without huge sacrifices on your part. I'll show you how in a few pages.

There we have it: three completely different attitudes toward money:

Group One, **I Will! I Will! I Will!** people, are aware of how wealth can grow and know they can make it happen. They are usually in business or a highly paid profession. One of their objectives is to be sure their children can handle money wisely rather than taking it for granted. Their lessons can actually be looked at as "Life Lessons." They are, in fact, almost the same.

> *In order to become an Automatic Millionaire, you've got to accept the idea that regardless of the size of your paycheck, you probably already make enough money to become rich.*
>
> – David Bach[12]

Group Two, the **Money is Frightening** folks, might be quoted as saying, "Money is the root of all evil" (a misquotation from the Bible, by the way). Some don't ever want to look at their finances; others just expect to be poor forever; and some hang on to every single dollar, worried that poverty will soon pound on their door.

Group Three, the **I Have a Plan** people, are often those who have chosen careers that may not necessarily pay enormous sums. They might be hourly or blue-collar workers, laborers, social workers, teachers, or those creative souls whose financial rewards come sporadically. But I Have a Plan folks know that they don't have to be among the Money is Frightening group. After all, they have thought about it and have developed a strategy. If it is sound (not one that could hurt others or that is rooted in a shaky moneymaking scheme) it will usually work.

No matter what type you are personally, your children should be in the I Have a Plan group. They have the most important ingredient to make long-term plans work: they have TIME.

Are You Learning From Experience?

One accountant I often talk to quotes some of his clients who say, "The trouble with personal experience is: I can't afford any more."

His clients aren't the only ones. For thousands of years, learning by that method alone has been unreliable.

William C. King, an author and a publisher in the early 1900s, brings up the problem. In his book *Portraits and Principles of the World's Great Men and Women*, King discusses the fact that learning by experience sometimes means we learn too late:

> It is well, then, to remember that there is no teacher like experience, nor any lessons so impressive and so costly as hers.
>
> Very many, indeed, will learn at no other school, and all of us have, at some time, to take more or less lessons there. Yet it is neither wise nor safe to depend entirely on what you may learn from her for you will find that the knowledge gained there, however valuable, often comes too late to be of benefit to you in this life and serves only to remind you of previous mistakes. Be willing, therefore, to learn from others.[13]

Many of us, either because of the economy, abrupt changes in retirement plans, or our own lack of action, have realized that it's going to be difficult to retire well even though we wish fervently that we could. Like King says, experience alone can be a costly teacher.

If you personally are worried, take a little money this very month and head for a financial planner so you can get the benefit of his or her knowledge. You may have to move it into high gear. But you'll get on track and you'll feel better.

Going to a financial advisor may be difficult. I couldn't summon up the courage many years ago to follow my own advice. I knew we could use help but never even made an appointment. Here were my reasons:

1. I didn't think we had enough money to pay for a consultation (although I never even called to find out what the going rate was).

2. I thought I would have to collect all of our family's income, budget, bills and goals before going in. I told myself I was too busy to gather that information. (I am fairly sure that a copy of our tax return would have been enough to start.)

3. But most importantly, I was embarrassed. My husband and I made very little money as teachers. I honestly did not want anyone to know how little we had to live on, much less how little we might have to invest.

So I let it go. I did read books on finances and we saved everything we could. During our early family years we went into the rental business and with help from our parents saved for and made down payments on houses. That has turned out just fine because my husband was an excellent maintenance man and landlord. But there were some choices we might have made differently had we sought good professional advice.

Call, please. That call and even one meeting might change your future.

> 'Save' – the sum of all financial planning wisdom in one word.
>
> – Dr. Phil DeMuth[14]

In the meantime, realize that your children could be asking different questions of their financial advisors when they are your age, questions like, "Where should I invest this extra money that I have accumulated?" rather than, "How will I ever be able to live if I have to quit working?"

We can gently teach our children that not only is:

"A penny saved a penny earned,"

but also that:

Time can turn our pennies into a quiet fortune.

Chapter Four:

How This Whole Thing Works

None of this stuff I've been echoing about compound interest is new. Some of us first learn about it in school.

I got the BIG lesson from an uncle who sat down with my husband and me almost 40 years ago, trying to make believers of us. But even though we "got it," the lesson eventually faded. You see, my uncle was selling mutual funds and I was skeptical of salespeople, even a well-meaning relative. We did start putting some money aside, but when the monthly minimum we needed to contribute went up (his company found the paperwork too time-consuming for our tiny investment) we quit.

We hadn't really absorbed the importance of compounding interest. Besides, our children were growing and their needs were growing also.

Many Americans face similar circumstances. We know that saving will pay off in the end, but life just seems to get in the way. We have lots of time, don't we? Right now our daughter needs braces and our son has asked for new basketball shoes. Everyone at work goes out to lunch so we really shouldn't pack a sandwich on Mondays and Wednesdays, should we? Just think of all the networking we'd miss. Some big-ticket items we have needed for a few years are on sale right now; better buy them. Besides, savings returns are so low … how could it possibly be worthwhile to save a little bit of money?

Anyway, we're just too busy to set up that automatic account with an investment company right now; we'll get on it next month. Really, we will.

And so it goes. Unless we truly understand that there's a unique reward to saving and investing most of us won't start saving seriously until reality slaps us in the face.

Far too many people in their 50s and 60s say, "If only I had started saving earlier … if only I had known!" So we begin tucking away every dollar we can. Maybe we'll never catch up to the amounts we might have had. But it's important to start, even if we're older. Having money in the bank brings a real sense of relief. Next time our country goes through another downturn or recession, we will have enough to feel okay. We might be able to travel a bit, to buy that great car we've always dreamed of, or just to know that we'll be able to pay our heating bills and enjoy some of the comforts of life.

For us, the future is here: if only we had known about the power of time.

Our children need our help to find out early about that power. The story you just read called "Two Good Buddies" points it out. Mark sacrificed early in his life and invested $2,000 each year. At first that $2,000 was hard to come by. He did extra work to earn it, but he knew what the rewards would be. He knew that eventually his investment would more than make up for what other retirement funds would not provide.

Robbie, when he began to think about retirement, realized that he would have to invest almost $2,000 per month – close to $20,000 a year – to get similar results. Now that would be a sacrifice. In fact, on his salary it was probably going to be impossible. While Mark's 40s and 50s were fairly easy financially, Robbie's would be an arduous race to accumulate money for his later years. How much easier, how much more leisurely, it would have been if only he had started earlier.

> *To the building of an estate there must always be the beginning. That start may be a few pieces of gold or silver which a man diverts from his earnings to his first investment.*
>
> *– George Clason[15]*

What's So Interesting About Interest?

How can we make sure our children learn smart money habits? We can make sure that we, personally, understand exactly how compounding interest works. Then we can lead our children toward that understanding.

Just as our children should learn to add and subtract by using their brains before they start using calculators, we ourselves should see how compounding works on paper, not just with a quick calculation. A story is okay, but true understanding must be deeper if we are to keep and teach the lesson.

Here's a chart that shows you how the Mom and Pop Plan can actually work. Spend some time looking it over: you will quickly understand its power. You'll see how small sums added slowly can grow into half a million dollars.

Now, DO NOT turn past this chart! I know: lists and columns of numbers drive many of us crazy. Unless we're accountants. Or nerds. Or rich.

But we do have a chance of being in that third group – the relatively well off at least – and especially of teaching our children how to grow in wealth. We need to understand that with compounding interest big gains don't come until later. Growth seems slow at first, and it is. That may be why so many of us get discouraged during the early years. But oh, the amazing jumps later on when our balances grow more rapidly each year!

So go ahead – see what I'm talking about. Spend five minutes looking at this chart. You'll see the massive shifts that occur as the account ages along with our kids.

The Mom and Pop Plan Chart

How a little child can start with $500 and get to $500,000

Age	Start Year With	Added Monthly	Equals Added Yearly	Total to Invest for the Year	7% of Total to Reinvest	Ending Total for Year
5	500	0	0	500	35	535
6	535	25	300	835	58	893
7	893	25	300	1,193	84	1,277
8	1,277	25	300	1,577	110	1,687
9	1,687	25	300	1,987	139	2,126
10	2,126	25	300	2,426	170	2,596
11	2,596	50	600	3,196	224	3,420
12	3,420	50	600	4,020	281	4,301
13	4,301	50	600	4,901	343	5,244
14	5,244	50	600	5,844	409	6,253
15	6,253	50	600	6,853	480	7,333
16	7,333	50	600	7,933	555	8,488
17	8,488	50	600	9,088	636	9,724
18	9,724	50	600	10,324	723	11,047
19	11,047	50	600	11,647	815	12,462
20	12,462	50	600	13,062	914	13,976
21	13,976	50	600	14,576	1,020	15,596
22	15,596	50	600	16,196	1,134	17,330
23	17,330	50	600	17,930	1,255	19,185
24	19,185	50	600	19,785	1,385	21,170
25	21,171	50	600	21,771	1,524	23,295
26	23,295	100	1,200	24,495	1,715	26,210
27	26,210	100	1,200	27,410	1,919	29,329
28	29,329	100	1,200	30,529	2,137	32,666
29	32,666	100	1,200	33,866	2,371	36,237
30	36,237	100	1,200	37,437	2,621	40,058
31	40,058	125	1,500	41,558	2,909	44,467
32	44,467	125	1,500	45,967	3,218	49,185
33	49,185	125	1,500	50,685	3,548	54,233
34	54,233	125	1,500	55,733	3,901	59,634
35	59,634	125	1,500	61,134	4,279	65,413
36	65,413	150	1,800	67,213	4,705	71,918
37	71,918	150	1,800	73,718	5,160	78,878
38	78,878	150	1,800	80,678	5,647	86,325

39	86,325	150	1,800	88,125	6,169	94,294
40	94,294	150	1,800	96,094	6,727	102,821
41	102,821	175	2,100	104,921	7,344	112,265
42	112,265	175	2,100	114,365	8,006	122,371
43	122,371	175	2,100	124,471	8,713	133,184
44	133,184	175	2,100	135,284	9,470	144,754
45	144,754	175	2,100	146,854	10,280	157,134
46	157,134	200	2,400	159,534	11,167	170,701
47	170,701	200	2,400	173,101	12,117	185,218
48	185,218	200	2,400	187,618	13,133	200,751
49	200,751	200	2,400	203,151	14,221	217,372
50	217,372	200	2,400	219,772	15,384	235,156
51	235,156	250	3,000	238,156	16,671	254,827
52	254,827	250	3,000	257,827	18,048	275,875
53	275,875	250	3,000	278,875	19,521	298,396
54	298,396	250	3,000	301,396	21,098	322,494
55	322,494	250	3,000	325,494	22,785	348,279
56	348,279	250	3,000	351,279	24,590	375,869
57	375,869	250	3,000	378,869	26,521	405,390
58	405,390	250	3,000	408,390	28,587	436,977
59	436,977	250	3,000	439,977	30,798	470,775
60	470,775	250	3,000	473,775	33,164	506,939

Total Invested: $85,500   **Total Made: $420,938**

MILESTONES AND COMMENTS

AGE 5:   Parents start a small mutual fund.

AGE 17:   Interest has become more than the yearly contribution.

AGE 18:   Child is a high school graduate with $11,000 in account.

AGE 21:   Child takes over payments. Making more than $1,000 interest yearly.

AGE 30:   1/2 way to age 60. Only $40,000 in account. A lot happens soon.

AGE 43:   Interest is 4 times what is contributed yearly.

AGE 48:   Over $200,000 in account.

AGE 54:   Way over $300,000 by now. Increasing rapidly.

AGE 57:   Going up by $100,000 every 3 years now.

AGE 60:   Over half a million dollars. Much more if interest is higher.

The Parameters of This Mom and Pop Plan

We're assuming that you have put aside $500 to start a mutual fund account for your child when she turns five. (Wow! That early? Why? … I'll show you in a few pages. And don't worry too much if you don't have $500. We'll talk about that also.)

Between ages five and ten you contribute $25 monthly to the account.

As your child ages you increase the monthly contribution. Between 11 and 20 you contribute $50 per month. By this age it's absolutely possible for your child to help chip in for that $50 if she understands the reward, even though the need for gas money and the reality of college expenses are ever-present.

At 21 your child takes over the mutual fund contributions completely. She gradually adds to the amount she invests.

Here's the summary of what you and then your child will invest in the example as time goes on. I have chosen amounts that should be feasible, despite all the other obligations of parents and young people.

Ages:		
	5-10	$ 25/month
	11-20	$ 50
	21-25	$ 50 (Child takes over at age 21)
	26-30	$100
	31-35	$125
	36-40	$150
	41-45	$175
	46-50	$200
	51-60	$250

During all of this time our example will average a return of seven percent on the investment. (This average spans many years, as you can see. The actual investment will often gain more, but it will also lose money during other years. These numbers are for purposes of illustration since we need to have a basis with which to begin.)

This chart presents a picture of investing with a method that most of us will be able to accomplish. Because money is often tight for parents in their early marriage-with-children days, it starts with small amounts. But it should be possible to save $25 each month or to earn that much extra with a small job or overtime.

Beginning an investment account for a five-year-old might seem absurd until we really look at and compare the numbers. If our child waits just 13 more years to begin investing, instead of beginning with $500 she would need to start with $10,000 to accumulate the same amount over time. That's hard for many of us, especially with the high costs of college looming. If an account isn't begun until even later, this is what our child would have to start with to achieve the same results as our "super early" chart:

Age: 30 $40,000
        40    $102,000
        50    $235,000

By these ages the hope for a significant return might be almost gone unless there's a big influx of money from some other source. (Back to our Rich Uncle Plan?)

I understand that $500 may seem to be an impossible amount. In a later book I'll show you how you can overcome that hurdle. If you are a grandparent you might be in a position to help out. A gift for the grandchildren toward a real start of investing might be appreciated for a long, long time.

In the Mom and Pop Plan you can see that the responsibility shifts from parents to child and that the amount contributed monthly slowly grows from $25 to $250. This is not the method that brings the fastest actual growth but it is feasible for most people: as our children age their own salaries will normally increase and their financial obligations of child rearing will eventually decrease.

> **Establish the habit of saving and investing so that it becomes as natural as breathing. You just do it without thinking.**

■ "The End of the Chart" Story

The actual Miracle of Compounding Interest appears toward the end of this chart. This is the lesson that is most important: it is easy to become discouraged in the early years of investing as we earn only small amounts like $35 one year, $58 the next. We might look at the totals in five years and think, "Heck, that account has only $2,000 in it. It's not growing very fast and we could really use that money now." That is when we must have a solid understanding of how compounding works:

Using our seven percent example we can see that small and steady contributions give our child $40,000 when she turns 30. That's almost half way to retirement and it's not much – even though it is more than most people have saved. Does that mean our daughter will reach 62 with about double that amount, somewhere around $80,000? Absolutely not.

Compounding interest (remember, I'm using the word "interest" even though these are really "earnings") as well as more generous contributions – up to $3,000 per year during the last ten years – will bring rapidly increasing totals:

At age 30:	$ 40,000	
By age 40:	$103,000	
By age 50:	$235,000	*(A $200,000 jump in 20 years)*
By age 55:	$348,000	*(A $113,000 jump in 5 years)*
By age 58:	**$437,000**	***(Faster increases. Now they are almost $100,000 every 3 years)***

As time goes on, the totals increase much faster.

Time + Interest = A Little Miracle Down the Line

█ Lessons Learned

The chart you just looked at demonstrates one of the most important concepts in the fairly simple accumulation of money. Of all the lessons your child may learn in school or out in regard to personal finance, this is the most crucial:

Money can grow if it is invested.

It can grow exponentially if it is invested early.

Time and Compound Interest are the keys.

We adults can help our children tremendously if we keep these things in mind:

1. As parents and grandparents we have enormous influence over our children's habits. We can gradually and easily teach them to spend and save sensibly, even while we teach them the other important lessons of life.

2. Even if we personally did not get these lessons as young people – especially if we did not – we can learn money lessons today and carry on. We'll feel much better ourselves if we begin a real savings habit while our children do the same.

3. Most people will not have careers that pay breathtaking salaries. And that's okay; to do what you love in a career is usually more important than working just because the salary is large. No matter what we do for a living, if we make some smart choices we will be far more secure as we reach the time when our working days come to an end.

4. If we teach our children about wise financial choices they will be able to do what they love while at the same time accumulating significant sums for later on; often they will feel very little sacrifice.

▋ Questions and Answers

Time and again I have heard people say they know they should have begun saving money earlier in life. As they explain why they didn't, these thoughts emerge:

Q: We think we need a large amount of money to begin investing.

A: We can start saving and investing with as little as $25.

Q: We think investments are risky and we're afraid of losing our money.

A: Some investments are indeed risky. Some are safe. Most are somewhere in the middle. Not saving or investing is the most financially risky of all.

Q: We are not sure how to start (or even where to find out how to start) investing.

A: Yes, the world of finances is complicated. But each one of us can start simply. The most powerful idea is that, although we may know very little, we can have plenty of smart people working for us in a matter of minutes. (More about that in the next book.)

Q: Our debt (school, mortgage, credit card) is already overwhelming. It's tough to think about taking on the obligations of saving.

A: Even if we are struggling with debt ourselves, the more steps we take toward solid ground the stronger we will feel. Saving a little money is one of those steps. A year from now or even less we'll know we are heading toward solvency.

Q: The economy and the future are so uncertain. How can we really plan for them?

A: Yes the future is uncertain, but only if we forget that the economy (and our own finances) almost always go up-down-up-down and on and on. How do we plan for that? We plant the seeds that will let our fortunes weather the droughts – or the storms – that will inevitably occur.

Q: We think it will take so much time to start an investment plan (learning, organizing, researching, putting finances in order) that we put it off month after month, year after year.

A: You don't need to take full-blown courses in investing. Just start. I'll tell you more about how later on. You will want to learn a bit more as you go on, but for now, START. More understanding can come later on as you get interested.

Q: We are already just hanging on. How could we ever set money aside?

A: It's true: many of us are "just hanging on" much of our lives. We call it living paycheck-to-paycheck. Learning to save a bit of money, even a few dollars a month in the beginning, will be tough at first. But soon it fills us with an incredible sense of pride and power. Then the paycheck-to-paycheck treadmill can come to an end.

Q: Our spouses can't seem to get on board.

A: An uncooperative spouse is a problem, and one that requires plenty of honest communication. One place to start might be by reading the first chapters of this book together. You may have to set money aside on your own just to get the ball rolling. And there's good news – according to *Money* magazine, "Research from the University of Missouri finds when one partner starts saving, the mate almost always gets on track too."[16] Without a doubt, having two people in a marriage working toward the same goal is best.

Q: If we personally haven't made great financial decisions, how can we possibly teach our children?

A: Teaching our children how to save is not the same as teaching our children calculus. We don't have to be experts; we only need a little clue and a good attitude. In fact, the best teachers may be parents who struggle themselves. Imagine the thrill of both parent and child trying to save two percent of their income – then three – then four – all the while talking about decisions and difficulties, rewards and triumphs. This could actually become fun!

If you have not yet mastered saving and investing, you may be the **best teacher of all**. Do not forget that.

> *The portfolios of people who trade the most underperformed the holdings of those who trade the least by an amazing 7.1 percentage points per year.*
>
> – Jason Zweig[17]

▌ Before this Book Ends

My examples are simple and not necessarily representative of what we will need later on; I know that. But they are accurate in the sense that they are examples of the power of Time and Compounding when the two are combined.

Straightforward ways of looking at compounded earnings (interest) are available. An algebraic equation of the Time Value of Money is relatively simple if you're into algebra. Websites show the results of compounding with the press of one key. But we should personally calculate the actual year-by-year growth of a small bit of money at least one time before we rely on quick ways to do this for us.

In Book Two, called *Learn, Invest, Teach*, I will show you how to teach this method of calculation to your children when they are old enough to understand. We will let them visually create their own fortunes. If a child does more than hit a key and watch an automatic result pop up, the impression becomes far more permanent. At least once, your child needs to experience the concept of slow – really slow – growth. It's important: that lesson will stay.

I have not discussed taxes in these manuals, nor will I mention the hundreds of investment options out there. I will give you one simple and highly recommended way to invest. Other options can all come later if you want to explore further.

The purpose of these books is to prove that you can help your children become so financially secure that no storm can throw them off course. Meanwhile, you too can learn these lessons and apply them to your own finances if need be.

The example in the Mom and Pop chart grows at seven percent consistently. This is only an example, but it is relatively close to a yearly average growth rate of the stock market. But even a return of one percent higher can make a huge difference. We'll see more about that particular phenomenon in the next two books.

Even though accountants, financial advisors, bankers and economists may have varying theories on what are the most lucrative ways to invest, they all agree with Professor Colin Fullenkamp of Duke University:

> "It's essential that you put time on your side by investing sooner rather than later and making a long-term commitment to regular investing." [18]

It's easy to start. It's easy to teach. It could almost be called the lazy person's way to riches. As we age we need to know a little more about investing (mainly, how to keep investments that return a decent amount but that get safer as we get older) but at first we just have to:

START ...
The earlier the better.

▌ What's Coming Next

BOOK TWO

Learn, Invest, Teach

- Find out what almost all financial advisors tell us to do
- Learn how easy it is to follow their advice
- Teach your children
- Get the kids started
- Make a difference in your own situation

BOOK THREE

It's So E.A.S.Y. for Young People

- See what your kids will learn about money – things most of us never learned when we were young
- Give the book to all the young people you care about
- Watch them grow in self-confidence and security

BOOK FOUR

The VIPs: Very Important Parents and Grands

Because you are your child's most important teachers, you'll read these few pages for ideas to get your kids and grandkids on the road to their own fortunes.

This book, *A Powerful Force*, is over. It's not long, but the ideas are really, truly important. They're important not just for you, but for every young person and parent you know.

Most financial books are crammed with advice about every single aspect of personal finances. They are often overwhelming. They are too easy to put aside and ignore because they're boring or intimidating or ... well, you name it.

That's why I've kept this book short. I want you to know that almost everyone can become wealthy by using just one idea:

Money compounded is, indeed, a powerful force.

WHAT CAN YOU DO NOW?

Read the next three books. They are for you, but they are also for both your kids and your parents. When you have finished reading take a step right away to let the magic begin. It's crazy how easy it is to put off saving and investing. It's even more amazing how easy it is to start! So go ahead...take a few steps toward those blessed feelings of security for you and your family.

Then do something even better: loan this volume to someone you know who could use it. When they return it, loan it to someone else, and then someone else. Spread the word that we don't have to remain poor forever. (Actually, better yet, buy a copy for them so you can keep yours around for that occasional look-through.)

I'm so glad you're here. It means your financial future will feel fine.

Book Two
Learn, Invest, Teach

Chapter One:

The Basics of Investing

One: A Savings Account
Two: Automatic Deposits
Three: Mutual Funds

That's all it takes, three steps. The process of investing can be very simple and it's almost identical whether you are thinking about yourself or your children. First, you gather some money together. Then you put it into a place where it has a good chance of growing over time. Regularly, and automatically, you add more.

These books are designed as companion volumes to help both you and your children learn a few basic lessons:

- Why we save and invest.

- How to save and invest.

- How your kids can be confident about money matters, knowing they are doing something that is both natural and exceptional.

You can teach the "how" and "why" to your children by spending a little time reading this information. The third essential, though, comes intuitively from you: learning to be confident about money happens when you have a saving and investing plan for yourself.

There's something really rewarding about being able to keep some of our hard-earned money and watching it grow. The sense of comfort you gain will make all the difference in your peace of mind. You'll be on the right track and you'll feel confident with that knowledge. Your assurance passes through to the kids.

Even though our country is notorious for low savings rates (as low as zero percent and into the negatives in the years preceding the recession that started in 2007) your family will not be among the miserable statistics.

This isn't complicated: you don't need to know anything about economics before you begin to grow your own nest egg; people have been doing it for centuries. In fact, the term "nest egg" comes from farmers who, when gathering eggs to sell or eat, would leave one egg in the nest. That way another chicken would hatch soon, ensuring that more eggs would always be available. Simple idea.

Today our nest eggs are in the form of investments. If we gather our money (by getting paid) then put just one little bit aside (our nest egg) we'll always have something that will grow and produce more. Instead of chickens, of course, we own parts of the world of finance. Each company we own a portion of employs hundreds or thousands of workers so we essentially get the benefit of all that labor. Those companies will bring a little more wealth to us. Bit by bit, our fortunes grow.

So, how do we go about owing part of this financial empire?

That answer could be a long and complicated one. If you are an economist or analyst you could talk for days about:

- How to invest.

- What advantages and disadvantages to consider.

- When to buy or sell a certain investment.

- Where to go for the best return.

- Why you need lots of analysis to be successful.

> *Unless you are extremely wealthy, just saving your money is not enough. You need your money to work as hard as you do, to produce a return of its own.*
>
> *– Jean Chatzky[19]*

They're right, there can be a lot to it. On the other hand, remember what Professor Connel Fullenkamp of Duke University said in the first book:

It's essential that you put time on your side by investing sooner rather than later and making a long-term commitment to regular investing.

Whether you know everything or not much, it's important to:

Just Start.
Take One Little Step.
Now.
Today.

How to Get Started
If Your Employer Will Help

If you are lucky enough to work for a company that provides matching funds for a 401(k) or other retirement plan, here's where you start. In fact, you absolutely should invest here.

What's a 401(k)? Remember back in *Book One, A Powerful Force*, when we talked about what happened to retirement? In the 1980s and 1990s, Defined Benefit Retirement (DBR) plans were phased out because companies knew those DBRs weren't economically feasible for them. The plans were replaced in large part with 401(k)s.

In a 401(k) the employer:

- Offers different kinds of investment funds to the worker.

- Puts the burden of planning for retirement on the worker.

- Often matches dollar-for-dollar what the worker contributes, up to a certain limit. Basically, the company still helps to provide a retirement plan, but does it at the front end and no longer is obligated to pay the employee or the employee's survivors after he or she has quit working.

Now that's good in a sense because very few people these days will work for the same company for a lot of years, as they did a few generations ago. With a 401(k) an employee's retirement fund can move from job to job, with a fairly simple transfer.

But here's the caveat: now we, the employees, are totally responsible for our own decisions. Social Security will certainly not be adequate to fund our later years. In addition, our employers will no longer decide how much to take out of our paychecks for our retirement, or which investments to make in our names, or when to switch those investments around. Now every single decision is up to us.

And that's where the problem comes. Many people simply are paralyzed with indecision. Have you ever looked at a list of funds available to you in your company's 401(k), spent twenty minutes trying to decipher what it's all about, then tossed the sheet aside in confusion (or disgust) thinking you'll look at it later? Lots of us have.

Here's a better solution:

- Talk to the human who is in charge of all this for your company.

- Get some advice.

- Sign up for something: some fund, some amount of money to contribute.

- Sign the beneficiary form now. You'll need your beneficiary's full legal name, birth date, and Social Security number, so have these with you.

- Walk away proudly, knowing that you did it!

You can always change the fund later. You can always adjust the amount you're saving. You can always take time to understand more when you have an extra hour or two (or month or two).

> *Over 70% of workers making between $30,000 and $50,000 will save if they have a retirement plan at work. Less than 5% will save if they have to open an IRA on their own.*
>
> *— The Aspen Institute Initiative on Financial Security event Working Towards a Secure Retirement: Strengthening Our Nation's Savings System*

But you will never regret having taken action today.

When you get your first 401(k) statement you might just decide to check on that list of options: does anything look better for you? Just knowing that you're really investing will make a difference in your interest level and your understanding. You'll learn more as time goes on and you may make changes, but please do not let any more precious matched money pass you by.

What if You're On Your Own?

Most of us don't work for companies with matching 401(k) plans, though. For us, it's every bit as critical to set up a retirement plan if we're on our own. It's even more important, because we are not going to be offered free matching money to start a retirement account. We need to get on it right now.

We'll talk here about ways to get into investing if your employer doesn't offer a retirement plan, or if you're interested in starting another fund, either for yourself or for the kids. Whether we're talking about you or your children, the steps to save and invest are basically the same. You may already be doing many of these things but I'll go over them in order. You will be teaching them to your children as they grow up.

Step One
Call Your Bank or Credit Union

You are, no doubt, familiar with banks, but ... credit unions?

Yes, in fact, credit unions are often excellent vehicles for housing some money. They offer savings accounts, they provide low-interest auto and other loans, and even though they have membership requirements such as where a person lives or works, those requirements are often looser than they once were. Almost everyone can find a credit union to belong to. So check them out.

Spend 15 minutes calling around or checking the Internet.

Find out which institution pays the highest interest on savings accounts, then tell your bank or credit union representative that you want to open one. That may take five minutes and $25 to $50.

If you're starting a savings account for a child you might be pleasantly surprised – quite a few banks will actually contribute the first $10 or $20 themselves.

That's it: Step One is done.

Step Two
Make Regular Deposits

Tell your representative that once a month you want a certain amount automatically moved from your main account into your new savings account. Make it as much as you can do without, even if it means a bit of budgeting. It might be $10, $25, or $100 a month, or far more. Automatic moves can take place between financial institutions if you ask, so your options are open. They'll help you set up any kind of transfer you ask for.

Now Step Two is done. You're almost an investor. You almost own part of a group of companies. Not quite yet, but soon.

You'll need some time before completing Step Three, but the more you move into savings every month the closer you are to becoming an investor. You may soon be able to think of yourself as a powerhouse of finances … really.

Step Three
Mutual Funds – Get One

Mutual funds are vehicles that allow people to invest in stocks, bonds, real estate and other areas even if they don't have large amounts of money at any one time. They are good for people who want their money to grow at a decent rate but who may not have either the expertise or the time to manage all the details of independent investing.

In the United States mutual funds began in the 1890s to encourage people to take advantage of opportunities in the nation's and the world's economies. Brilliant people set up and manage mutual funds (okay, we hope they are at least knowledgeable and sort of smart) and we pick the ones we want to invest in based on our level of risk tolerance and other factors.

Many types of mutual funds exist, all of which make money in different ways. If we choose stock – also called "equity" – funds, for example, our money buys slivers of companies, most of which (again, we hope) earn a bit more this year than they did during the last. We get some of the profit, either by increased share value, dividends, or a combination of the two.

▮ Why Mutual Funds?

Of course there are other vehicles you could choose to invest in but these are excellent for starting out. They are the single investment that virtually every financial advisor suggests for beginners. Even Warren Buffett, one of the world's most successful investors, says index funds (mutual funds which mimic certain benchmarks like the S&P 500, for example) are an ideal way for most of us to invest.

The world of finances can be complicated. To invest in almost anything else and earn a decent return you either need to have a large amount of money or a depth of knowledge that most people don't possess when they begin. Mutual funds are clear-cut and inclusive. You can see the companies you are buying, past returns, and the relative safety of each fund.

A few decades ago certificates of deposit were excellent and safe investments for the average American. At that time they returned an insured 12% and more. Wow! But today a CD owner can only hope to earn 1% or 2%, not even enough to keep up with inflation. So we turn to the stock market through mutual funds.

Mutual funds are not insured. But while some of them may be riskier than others they also have the potential to give us an excellent return. Others are much safer because their main objective is safe growth of money. How do we know which is which? By doing three things:

1. First learn a little about them on Internet or through books or by talking to an accountant or a financial advisor.

2. Make a phone call to a company that sells mutual funds. Talk to a representative.

3. After he or she makes some suggestions about what kind of funds to look at, ask how to get the prospectus and more information.

Now, if you really hate the idea of financial stuff or if you're afraid that all this will be too time consuming, don't quit now. In just a few pages I'll tell you how to get started before you learn "everything you need to know." Or much of anything, for that matter. Getting started is by far the most important thing, and you can do it with the help of an expert. Read on!

Learning about mutual funds could take a bit of time if you're new to them but the process will be intriguing as you realize what's in store. Do this investigating while your savings account is growing. You'll need at least $500 to $1,000 to start, depending on which fund you decide to invest in, so you'll probably have some time to learn.

You will have many options about which company and what fund(s) to pick. This can be an exciting process. Look at it as though you have a much anticipated vacation coming up and you want to find the perfect place to go: will it be an island or the mountains, a bed-and-breakfast, a fine hotel, a theme park or camping? Will you want to fly or drive? When we plan our vacations we think about the advantages and disadvantages of each possibility. Do the same with your decisions about the greatest (and hopefully the longest) vacation of all – your post-working years.

Ways to Learn About Mutual Funds

Several sources are available to help you learn quickly about mutual funds:

- Get some basics from a non-biased source. You might look up Mutual Funds in Wikipedia, for example, and learn a lot in just a few clicks. You'll be able to connect to links that discuss all kinds of topics, including the top ten companies in the U.S. that sell mutual funds. This will give you insight into the different philosophies, funds, and fees of these companies. But be aware that the lists may not be completely up-to-the-minute.

- Using only a source like Wikipedia may be a bit risky. It is written by the general public so may contain some errors that won't exist in published reference books. Check out Morningstar.com after you have learned a few things about what to look for in a mutual fund. Morningstar offers highly respected and neutral analyses of every mutual fund available. You can start with a free trial period and may not need more. Most libraries also offer it, in print or online – all you'll need is a library card, and maybe not even that.

- You can just search the Internet for "Mutual Fund Families" and you'll find updated information about rankings, fees, performance, etc.

  Fidelity and Vanguard are among the largest and best-known families (companies) and their fees are among the lowest. T Rowe Price is also a no-load fund family that comes recommended by advisors, and there are more.

Low fees make a real difference for your future. I'm quoting from the Wall Street Journal here: "According to Vanguard Group, over a 40-year career, someone who invests 9% a year of a salary that starts at $30,000 into a balanced fund and pays 0.25% a year in fees will save 20% more than a person who pays 1.25% in fees."[20] So investor "A" might end up with $500,000 while investor "B" ends up with $600,000, just because of lower fees.

- You might want to visit the library or bookstore and pick up a book on investing. You'll be able to get detailed information that will serve you well, especially if you get more interested.

- Visit with people who know something. Don't just ask cousin Millie what she does, then plunge in. But if you ask her a few questions, then talk to four other investors, you'll probably learn something valuable from their experiences.

- Be cautious of tales of woe from friends. This often means the person did not know enough to keep investing when the market went down for a period, which it will. Or even worse, he or she may have actually sold everything during a downturn, completely eliminating the ability for the account to climb back up when times got better.

- Talk to an accountant or a financial advisor if you want to. They know a lot, will give you generally very solid advice, and can take care of paperwork for you. I'll tell you more about them later.

- Play around! Spend some time looking for information that fits your needs. Don't worry if things seem complicated (all those statistics!) Move on to articles that make sense to you. Try to get information from impartial sources as often as possible.

▊ Some Terms You'll Learn

Just as if you were looking for a house to buy, you'll want to find out some specifics first. With a house you ask how many bedrooms it has, when it was built, if it's close to a busy highway, or if it has a new roof and plumbing. With mutual funds you'll want to pay some attention to terms such as:

- Index or actively managed
- Load or no-load
- High or minimal fees
- Diversification

You will learn the differences between:

- Small, medium, and large cap companies
- Value vs. growth stocks
- High, medium, and low risk vs. potential return

If you want, you can just enter the words into your web browser and definitions will pop up.

Generally, most advisors suggest that beginning investors look for funds that are:

Index	These follow the markets instead of trying to out-earn them.
No-load	These funds don't charge a commission when buying or selling.
Minimal Fees	Some companies charge higher fees than others. Fees make a big difference in the long run returns you'll get.

A computer search will give you a connection to all kinds of information. Phone calls will also bring you a wealth of people to ask questions of: each company wants your business, so they are more than happy to give you individual help. In addition, they can't make unwarranted claims. Call and ask questions.

Talk to an accountant or a financial advisor if you want to. They know a lot. Be cautious of tales of woe from friends.

What the Heck is a Prospectus?

And Why Should I Read It?

A prospectus is a legally required document that will let you know the risks, objectives, holdings and operations of a mutual fund. A prospectus may look daunting at first glance but the important information is not complicated. Before you buy into a fund, you really should look at it. A phone call or Internet click will get you the prospectus. You'll feel much more in control when you know what you're buying.

> The way that people accumulate wealth is that they decide to save a significant chunk of their income. Most people of all income brackets don't do this, and that's why most people never accumulate any significant assets.
>
> – Zac Bissonnette[21]

▌ Are You Ready? Just Do It!

Now you're ready to actually become wealthy, or to set up a fund to help your child. You have saved some money. You have learned a few things. You have found out a bit about companies and funds that fit your risk tolerance and objectives.

If you choose to invest on your own and use an online broker such as Vanguard, call the company and ask them what to do. Or fill out their registration forms online. Use the money from your savings to begin the fund, and you're off and running. A representative can help you every step of the way.

You'll also want to keep contributing, so now you can set up an automatic transfer from your bank account to the mutual fund. Again, a phone call or online registration will work. Remember, the company should be extremely helpful because they want you to be satisfied, so use their advice about how to make things seamless.

And one last piece of advice on this step: don't ever, ever, ever think you're not rich enough to do this! Even if you start with only a small amount because you simply can't do more right now, you'll be amazed by next year how much better you feel about your financial future. I can almost guarantee you'll want to increase your contributions and will do it as soon as you possibly can.

Finally, Make That Mutual Fund an IRA

(Individual Retirement Account)

When you do talk to advisors and/or representatives you should probably tell them you want to set your mutual fund up as an IRA (Individual Retirement Account). IRAs are like 401(k)s, but you don't have to get them from your employer – they can be set up just for you, as long as you are earning money. (A child can't have an IRA until he or she actually earns some kind of wage, but a mutual fund is okay.) IRAs provide important tax advantages that can help you considerably in the long run.

Now, an IRA is simply a little container that your mutual fund sits in and that protects it from too many taxes; it's not the mutual fund itself, which could be any combination of stocks, bonds, or other investments. IRAs were set up by legislature to give you tax advantages so that you can save for retirement, not for a new car or a shiny diamond.

(If you do want to start a mutual fund account to save for something other than retirement, that's fine. You just won't put it into that IRA "container." With a regular mutual fund investment you'll still earn stock market-type profits, but you will pay taxes on them.)

IRAs come in different forms: Traditional IRAs, Roth IRAs, and a new type of fund called a "MyRA." The MyRAs have recently been established for people who know they need a retirement account but who don't make a lot of money. For most people, a Roth IRA is the best choice. In fact, by far the most highly recommended IRA is a Roth. Go online to see the differences between Traditional, Roth, and MyRAs.

Want to Learn With Less Effort?

Talk to an Advisor

If you're unsure of your ability to manage the jungle of options or if you feel more comfortable having an expert to talk to anytime you want, use a real person! You have probably driven past the offices of financial advisors hundreds of times. Instead of driving by tomorrow, stop in. In fact, call two or three to set up appointments. Pick a person and a company that put you at ease and that you would feel comfortable working with.

Ask anything you want to and look for clear answers to all of your questions, including questions about how they get paid. If you don't understand what they are saying, tell them. A good advisor will explain things clearly, and you deserve that. Fees will be higher than with online brokerages because of the personal attention you'll receive, but you will always have someone to talk face-to-face with, and that could be a big advantage. It's far better to pay a bit higher fee and **get started now** than it is to put off investing "until you have more time to learn."

Kinds of Advisors

FEE-ONLY

Fee-only advisors do not work under the umbrella of a particular investment company so they will be able to give you advice that includes many possible mutual fund families and other investments.

Strengths:

- They will generally be impartial and won't push to sell you on one particular company over another. They work for you.

To Consider:

- It's sometimes hard to find an independent financial advisor, especially in less urban areas.

- They sometimes get paid in a variety of ways. This may include charging you by the hour, or charging a percentage of the assets they manage for you, or even in some cases by "commission and fee." Ask about that and look for clear answers.

AFFILIATED

Affiliated representatives, or brokers, work under the auspices of a particular company. They know the savings and investment vehicles of their company thoroughly.

Strengths:

- They will be willing to see you at any time to discuss your goals.

- They don't charge you for their time.

- Their advice will be professional and backed by solid research.

To Consider:

- They will be able to direct you toward good funds but not all funds that are available.

- Their companies earn money by charging commissions and fees. Discuss what the long-term effects may be on your account balance.

FEE-BASED

"Fee-based means the brokers charge a fee in addition to collecting commissions."[22] It's a gray area at times, even among the professionals themselves, so ask questions about compensation. Your questions should be answered clearly by the advisor you choose.

Millions of people go it alone in the mutual fund world. And millions of others use established investment companies. Which should you do?

It depends upon your level of comfort, as well as your desire to learn on your own. Doing your own investing can be liberating, and over the years it can save you thousands of dollars in fees.

But make no mistake – you'll need to understand one of the most important concepts of the markets. It's not guaranteed that you'll make 7, 10, or 12% every year. The stock market will go up and you'll feel wealthy. Then it will plummet, maybe for several years, and your account will plummet as well.

If you have a good advisor you will be able to talk, plan, calm down, and keep your money in a decent fund. If you are likely to get nervous and sell during downturns, having an advisor will be well worth the fees.

In short, an advisor is as much a psychological counselor as a financial expert, helping you to keep building your quiet fortune during those times when you're worried. An advisor could be your most important asset.

That Old Savings Account

When you begin investing, what should you do with your rather depleted savings account? Keep it open! Keep a little bit going into it automatically. Even though savings accounts don't earn much interest at all, they are still a decent way to put money aside.

Maybe this time you'll be using that account to save for the dream vacation you've always wanted. Or how about making it a Christmas fund so the holidays don't hurt so much? Many people, including banking employees themselves, actually set up several savings accounts with a separate name for each. Most banks don't charge fees to set up these accounts, so use that power to be sure some of your shorter-term goals are getting a few dollars every month.

Of course there are ways to earn better interest safely without having to keep money in a savings account forever. Apps exist that will automatically sweep cash from checking accounts at certain brick-and-mortar banks into FDIC-insured savings accounts at online banks. MaxMyInterest.com is only one, and as soon as this book goes into print there will be many more. The point I'm making is that, if you haven't had time to look for these apps or that higher interest rate, just keep that savings account growing until you do.

▌ What If the Market Tanks?

Are you worried about losing money, as much of the nation did during the Great Recession that began in late 2007? What if you build up a large amount in a mutual fund and the economy goes down suddenly? Could that possibly happen again?

Well, here's my answer: don't wonder if the stock market will go down – know that it will. In fact, since the United States became an independent nation, we have had no less than 36 major panics, recessions, and depressions. And that number does not begin to include the smaller panics we have experienced. The U.S. has gone through an average of one big setback every 6½ years and experiences a "correction" several times a year.

So why on earth would we expose ourselves to that turmoil? For three very good reasons:

1. Yes, people who were invested in stocks often lost money. But each and every time it fell, the value of the market has climbed back up. Usually the climb has been rapid, quickly passing the previous high point. The key is to not pull out when there is a downturn. Keep investing.

2. People who were not invested in the market lost plenty, also. Those people often lost everything, though, including their jobs and their homes, because they did not have investments that could rise again.

3. If you invest automatically every month, then when stocks (hence, stock mutual funds) go down you now can get more shares with every deposit you make. A share in the fund that costs you $30 today may cost $20 during a big downturn. So you'll be able to buy more shares with your automatic deposits during those low months and your average price per share decreases. This is called dollar-cost averaging. When the value goes up again you'll own more shares than you might have if the price had not fallen.

It usually works out well as long as you understand that the market goes in cycles of rising and falling. You can consider a "fall" to be a time for bargain-basement prices if you own a good fund.

People who panic and pull their money out during a bear market always lose. Those are the people to avoid getting advice from – they are afraid to make downturns work in their favor. People who continue to invest in solid funds have almost always come out with a solid gain.

Remember; unless you actually need the money right when things are lowest, you really have not lost. On paper your portfolio may look pitiful, and that may be daunting. But if you keep your contributions going you are buying more for less, so it's like the stocks are on sale for a year or so. I admit that it's scary but when they rise you'll be back with more shares and the value of your fund (if it's a good quality one, not based on highly speculative investments) will be stronger.

> **Don't OWE Amazon, OWN Amazon.**
> **Don't OWE Whole Foods, OWN Whole Foods.**
> **One is crushing, the other is encouraging.**
> *– Terrie Drake*

As you get closer to retirement you obviously shouldn't take the risk of a big drop in value since you may, indeed, need the money at any moment. The representatives in your chosen company can give you information about how best to avoid a calamity. Generally, that will mean moving your money into a more secure fund that holds government bonds and other less risky investments.

Warren Buffett talked about lows:

> Whether we're talking about socks or stocks, I like buying quality merchandise when it is marked down.[23]

Chapter Two:

Need an Incentive?
Step Back Five Years

Do you think you're too busy to start today? Think back. Go back a year. Or two. Or five. What if you had started investing five years ago, maybe by putting just $100 into an investment portfolio every month?

You'd now have $6,000 or more and you'd be watching that amount grow every month.

What might you have had to give up to get to that stage? Maybe:

- A few hundred coffee shop drinks that you didn't need (and now regret having spent money on).

- That expensive outfit you bought years ago and only wore twice.

- Four must-have electronic devices that quickly became outdated.

- That fancy set of dishes you rarely use.

- The extra pounds you've put on by eating out a few too many nights every month.

But if you had started investing five years ago, what would you now have in addition to that $6,000 or more in your Quiet Fortune account? Perhaps:

- The knowledge that you'll be able to take care of yourself.

- A secret understanding that you'll have a more secure future.

- A habit that is now hard to break ... of smiling oh, so slightly to yourself when you think about your past money worries.

- Pride.

- Self-confidence.

- Security.

- An awareness of how many times a day advertisers try to make us believe we just can't live without their product, as well as the knowledge that what these advertisers really want, first and foremost, is to take your money and put it in their own accounts.

Only about half of workers in the U.S. age 55-plus say they have tried to calculate how much money they will need to save for retirement.[24] That may be because it's just plain scary. At least 50 percent of Americans save too little.

But you don't have to be in that group, nor do your children. Honestly, it feels so good to save some money regularly that, once we begin, we just know we have made ourselves stronger. We don't need to swallow hook, line, and sinker, the idea that we must look more gorgeous, act happier, or own more than the rest of the world, as advertisers try so hard to make us believe. What we do need is a slight shift from spending without thinking about it to saving steadily. Sure, we can have things, just maybe not so many of those extras we don't really need.

Economists and advisors usually tell us that we should save 10% to 15% of our salaries. That is definitely what we should aim for, but it can be a daunting amount if we have never saved and invested. If we need to we can start with just 2%, 3% or 4%. I promise you it will feel good, so good that within a year you'll be considering 6%, then 8%, and soon you will be at that most important 10% or more.

As Zac Bissonnette says:

> Once you get started with this [saving] plan you will find that, paradoxically, saving for retirement is actually more fun than spending on cool stuff. You'll have a feeling of power and control over your life. You'll sleep better at night knowing you're making progress toward financial power – the ability to be true to yourself.[25]

As Ordinary as Breathing

In the next chapter we'll show you simple ways to make saving and investing natural for your children, whether they're five years old or in college. We can teach them that saving is as ordinary a process as breathing and sleeping: it's just what we do.

If they start early our children will be able to live their lives as adults, confident that their financial futures will be secure instead of scary.

You'll be giving an immeasurable gift to your children if you teach them that a little bit should go into their "Forever" money, even while they plan excitedly what they'll do with the rest.

It's simple for kids. It means they won't be intimidated by the specter of future scarcity. They'll be excited about all the possibilities their futures will bring. You will be too.

Chapter Three:

Teach The Kids About Their Own Quiet Fortunes

The last chapters presented three steps toward a program of personal investing. You save some of your money, find a mutual fund that meets your goals, and continue automatically to put money into that mutual fund. Even if you can save only a few dollars at first, it's quite possible for you to begin investing. And it could turn into a fortune.

For your children the plan is basically the same. Actually, it's even easier. You already know about mutual funds so you won't have to search for much more advice when the time comes for your child to get into them.

We'll talk here about savings accounts and mutual funds and what might be good choices specifically for the kids. But we'll talk about some things that are even more important. You'll discover how easy it can be to help your children grow up with respect, not just for their money, but also for things that are even more important than a big bank account.

While your son learns to save, he'll be learning self-discipline. As your daughter earns the responsibility of making financial decisions, she will develop self-reliance. You'll notice lots of growing opportunities tucked into these financial messages.

As a parent your most important "financial advisor" role is to lead your child onto a path where saving and investing, thinking and sharing, become natural. Here we'll show you how to teach your young children what they need to know about money. As Napoleon Hill said:

> A human being's earthly destiny may be, and usually is, fixed for him through the influences of his childhood.[26]

So, let's get ready to have some real influence over our kids' destinies.

▌Influence

We parents make a big impression on how our children view the world. If we're excited about the future, our kids will likely view optimism as a philosophy to hang onto. If we treat people kindly, chances are good that they will refrain from judging others harshly. If we treat ourselves with respect our children will understand that we value our own lives and the experiences we can create.

The same goes with money. A parent who neither fritters away nor hoards money can help a young person understand that it, too, simply deserves respect. He learns to view it as a tool that helps people to get along in this world, to follow our dreams, to worry less about tomorrow's challenges, and to help others.

▌ The Quiet Fortune Lesson

We can begin teaching our children this broad-based view of money at almost any age. That's because everything starts with one very simple truth:

> Of all the money we make, a little bit of it should be for us. We should not squander, pay bills with, buy stuff with, or lose that little bit. It is for us to keep for later on.

You could call this The Lesson of Our Quiet Fortune:

Of all the money we make, some should be ours to keep.
It will grow quietly for the rest of our lives.

If you can convey that thought, you're fine. You'll have done your job in regard to your children's financial literacy.

▌Why Don't We Save?

"Of all the money we make, some should be ours to keep."

This concept seems fairly basic. In some countries it is. In China, for example, the per capita income is approximately one-sixth of that in the United States. But the Chinese save 20-30 percent of their incomes. They buy the basics but not that second or third TV or another, newer cell phone just because it's out there. Those are habits that we would be smart to consider.[27]

In the United States a dismally small percentage of people actually save some of their income consistently. There are plenty of reasons for this, and they reach back into the history of our nation as one of the wealthiest in the world. These reasons involve the availability of easy credit; good jobs during good times; low rates of interest, both in savings and in purchasing; awe-inspiring advertising budgets for companies to sell their products; and a general feeling that we will still be well off even if we do spend more than we make.

That is, until bad economic news hits. In the boom before 2008, for example, the United States was riding the tide of a housing bubble. We bought bigger homes with every expectation that their values would continue to rise. We bought appliances and cars and furniture and clothes on credit, and we saved little.

In fact, for several years before the Great Recession began the individual savings rate in the U.S. had actually dropped to below zero percent. Ouch! Even though we had been earning record amounts of money, as a nation of individuals we were tumbling into debt and saving nothing.

The Great Recession absolutely devastated millions of families. Their retirement incomes, their jobs, and their homes were all at risk. Out of the recession came thousands of financial advisors who echoed: "We must save three months' worth of salary for the bad times." As the recession continued that advice became "six months' salary" then, "We should save one year's salary for emergencies."

Oddly enough, despite the fact that our economy was worse than it had been for eighty years, personal savings rates for the nation climbed significantly during the recession, proving that saving money is possible even in tough times.

> **47% of the oldest boomers are at risk.**
>
> – Reported in 2010 by the Employee Benefit Research Institute (EBRI)[28]

What about just making a habit of saving some of our money for the inevitable time when we will need it? The people who had been saving and investing steadily before 2008 certainly did not get off without damage – many of them took a hit along with the rest of the nation. But if they were able to keep most of their money in solid investments their fortunes eventually rose again.

In addition, the people who had actually saved quite a bit of money during the good times now had the cash that would allow them to "make money on the buy." While others worried about paying their mortgages, savers could actually buy real estate and stocks at huge discounts, as well as all of the merchandise that businesses were forced to sell at rock-bottom prices. That expression, "The Rich Get Richer," held up during the Great Recession, at least for those who had prepared well.

By April 2010, stock market prices of the S&P 500, which had fallen 56% between peak (October 2007) and the trough (March 2009) were up 78% from the trough. By the end of 2014 the DOW (another measure of some of the companies in the overall stock market) had climbed to never-before highs. Most people were at least a little better off, but those who had had money to invest during the drops came out better than ever.

The habit of saving and investing can become natural for our next generation. We adults can teach them how important it is, and how easy.

Never Too Old?
Never Too Young!

The suggestions in this book begin when your child is as young as two years old. That's because good habits are easy to start when we're young, and because we want to capture the value of time. Most of you have children well beyond that age. Even if they are young adults by now, read all the steps; they contain basic and essential concepts. If your child is older you will just discuss the ideas in an appropriately mature way.

Here's a look at what is coming when your child is:

Very Young	• Get a piggy bank.
	• Start a minor's savings account.
2nd Grade or so	• Divide piggy's money into groups.
	• Start making a few decisions.
Middle School	• Learn about compound interest.
	• Get a mutual fund.
High School	Lots of money needs arise, so:
	• Student could get a part-time job.
	• Stay on track with mutual fund.
	• Learn the difference 1% can make.

In the real world you and your kids have hundreds of things going on. You teach your children everything, from how to brush their teeth to how to get along with others to how to deal with serious problems. This money stuff is only one of the many lessons you can instill. And it really is more of an attitude you'll pass on, like optimism and respect, hard work and generosity. It should involve only a couple of minutes every few months.

By the way, as I talk about your children you may notice that I refer to "him," "her," "family," and "Mom and Dad." This is only because our English language, global as it may be, does not contain words that are more inclusive. For example, there is no one pronoun that means "one child, either male or female." So I switch between "he" and "she."

Likewise, we do not have a concise way to describe the vast array of parent-child relationships in our country. "Family" seems to fit best. I am not just talking about a two-parent-with-at-least-one-child group. We're way past that: I wish we could come up with better words that can do the trick for all of our great arrangements. Oh well, you get the idea.

> I'm often asked, "At what age should a person start saving?" To me, that's similar to asking at what age you should start brushing your teeth. Well, when you have teeth to brush! So I say you should start saving and investing money from your 1st paycheck. Try saving 5% of every paycheck and then eventually increase your saving to 10%.
>
> – Eric Tyson[29]

▌ When Your Child is Small

Even before your child has any idea at all about money, you can help
her get on the way to saving.

One step you'll take is to buy a piggy bank. Or make a savings bank
out of an empty box and decorate it with family photos. Anything will
do, just get something that will safely hold loose change.

The next step will be to call your bank. Ask about their minors'
savings accounts. These are accounts that can be started in your
child's name, but the young person cannot access the money without
your approval. Banks only ask for small initial deposits, usually
around $25. Some banks even pay you to start one by making the first
deposit. Open an account and you're ready. It will take about 10-15
minutes and can often be done online or over the phone.

Now, when your little person has a birthday or celebrates a holiday,
instead of buying that one extra gift put a small amount into the
savings account.

Not many banks charge a service fee for a minor's savings account. If
yours does, start the bank account a few years from now. Baby's piggy
bank will do for now. Make sure it's a large one – you'll keep feeding
it and it should be ready to hold some genuine money, not just token
coins, if it's taking the place of a bank account for a while.

If the conversation ever comes up tell Grandma and Grandpa that
baby has a tiny savings account. If they think you're crazy just let
them know that you have set it up for the future. Tell them you
know how time can turn a small amount of money into a small
fortune. Chances are they'll congratulate themselves for having
raised a smart kid like you.

If they seem pleased and proud of your foresight, hand them a deposit
slip and tell them they are more than welcome to donate anytime.

▌More Than One Account

Your child won't know about her savings account for years. But she can get an idea about saving when you use her piggy bank. When you and your child stuff some coins into Piggy she'll figure out that it is worth taking a few seconds to put them in a safe place.

A few seconds should be all it takes. If you find a penny you can pick it up and say, "Oh good! Let's put this in your piggy when we get home." Then remember to do it. Just use a subtle example that you know the value of this penny. That's it.

Keep Piggy for savings. As your child gets older she will want a little money to spend. You might put a small spending box or bowl next to her piggy bank so she can have two "accounts." This way she will begin to understand that some money is for saving and some is for spending.

The piggy banks you can buy in stores serve their purpose: they show a child that it is good to have a place to put money. But as soon as piggy is opened up and the money is spent, the obvious – and wrong – lesson becomes that we save all our money so we can spend it. Not good.

Make piggy your child's safe place for saving money to keep. Do not open it until your child is older. The spending bowl will become the place your child can go to if she wants a few quarters to spend. As time goes on she'll keep putting one coin in the piggy bank when she puts another into the bowl. You don't even need to explain the difference between the coins if you don't want to: it's the difference between spending and saving that is important. Keep it easy, casual, and short. In time the concept will come.

> *Even when children are aware of price, it means much less to them than it does to an adult, who is able to compare the price to what it used to be, or to the price of rival products, or to the family's budget.*
>
> – Michael Schudson[30]

When Your Child Gets Older

By the time your child is somewhere around age seven he or she will have:

- A piggy bank for saving
- A spending bowl for spending
- A minor's savings account

It does not matter how much money is in the piggy bank and spending bowl but it's important that saving and spending money are separated. And if you haven't set up that minor's savings account yet, please do it now. In five or six years your child will be able to start investing and will need $500 to $1,000. It's so much easier to add ten or twenty dollars gradually over these early years than to wait until later. If Grandma and Grandpa are helping, so much the better.

I understand that it may seem absurd to think your child could start investing by the age of 12. On the surface, it's almost ridiculous. But let's jump ahead a few years. You know that the earlier an investment starts, the smaller the amount that will have to be invested. The difference between what a child will need to save to end up with one million dollars and what a 50-year-old will have to save is staggering.

In the United States around 64 percent of seniors don't have even close to enough money to retire. They will be forced to keep working well past the age when they would love to be doing something completely different. Do you know anyone like that? Inevitably, these seniors say they wish they had begun saving earlier but just didn't seem to be able to start.

Even as they say that, though, they probably don't realize that a $100 investment each month from a young age could have resulted in one million in an investment account today. That's the lesson and these are the gifts you will be giving your child if you set up that savings account:

- The understanding that saving is a natural part of earning.
- The immeasurable gift of time for compounding to work its magic.

A Sense of Control

People who learn how to save and divide their money into different uses often do better later on than those who do not feel as though they have control over their income.

That sense of control can happen as early as seven. This is the age when your child will become aware that the cash inside Piggy could buy something really cool. Suddenly "money" takes on a new importance when those toys and electronics could come home if he or she could only break into Piggy's stash. This is the perfect time to teach a big part of the Lesson of Your Forever Fortune.

Let's look at a common situation between parent and child at the store:

Ted: Dad, can I have this basketball?

Dad: It's great, but not right now.

Ted: Why, Dad? It's just what I've always wanted!

Dad: And it costs $29. That's a lot of money, Son.

Ted: But I have a lot of money! I've been saving money in my piggy bank forever. I bet I have tons more than that.

Dad: You just might, Teddy. When we go home we'll look. Let's do that tonight if we have time. But we'll have to do some talking and some planning. You can't just empty your bank and spend it all. I'll show you a few things that are sort of cool about the money you have saved.

I'm sure the basketball will be here later this week, but we'll ask at the counter if they can put one back for a few days.

> *Finally, there is the responsibility of raising kids who can handle financial matters. This goes beyond helping them set up a lemonade stand and open a bank account (good things, to be sure!) It means discussing money openly [and] teaching them calmly about financial decisions.*
>
> *– Daniel Solin*[31]

So the stage is set. Ted wants something that's far bigger than the treats he has bought so far using his "spending bowl" and he knows there is big money in his savings account called Piggy.

It's time to get rid of the piggy bank and design something that will last forever.

At this point when you talk to your children about money you can give them the sense of control that they will appreciate all of their lives. You don't have to wait for the "I want a basketball" conversation, but it's a good time to start.

At home begin by explaining that when we get money we use it for different things. Some of it should stay ours for a long, long time. (This is that compounding interest account we'll help our child start in a few years.) We should keep a portion to help others when they need help. Some of it could be for things we want and some of it for things we need.

Get out four paper plates or pieces of paper. Label each with a category that you have just mentioned. The labels you choose will depend upon your child's age and ability to understand. These terms will stick around for a while, so give it a little thought. Here are some ideas:

Group 1	Group 2	Group 3	Group 4
Spending $	Spend	Want Now	Spend
Saving For Something Special $	Save	Need Later	Save
Giving $	Give	Give to Others	Share
$ To Keep	Grow	Keep Forever	Invest
The bottom row will become your child's "Quiet Fortune" account. You might want to call it that.			

Any version of these terms will work as long as they work for you. For now I'll use Group Four, "Spend, Save, Share, and Invest" because I think Teddy is old enough to learn about the concept of investing.

The basketball fits into the first category, Spend, so that is what Teddy will be most interested in right now.

First, take the money from Teddy's spending bowl and dump it all onto the Spend plate. It was always meant for buying treats and your child will know it's only fair to make sure it can go toward what he wants.

Now get Piggy out and declare that he is just not sophisticated enough anymore. You could hand him down to a younger sibling or even break him open with a hammer (yep, break him): it's time to get rid of the idea that all of our money goes into one or two pots. By separating their money our children learn that they have the power to actually decide where some of their income will go.

You will have a pile of coins and some bills that were once in the piggy bank. It's time to divide. If your child wants to, put a quarter on each plate and do it again and again, using the same coin on each round.

If your child is old enough to understand and add denominations, talk about how much might go into each category. Here's a chance to discuss a little bit about the relative importance of each. Be sure no group is severely shorted but allow your child to make the decisions about how much goes where. At least ten percent of the money should stay in the Invest plate. (Some parents insist on as much as 50 percent; you can decide what should go there during your child's growing-up years.)

Now let's get back to Teddy and his basketball. He is probably anxious to know if he has $29 to buy it immediately. If the money is sitting on the Spend plate, great. If not, talk a little about the difference between spending and saving. Spend (for Teddy) will be to use right away on that basketball and save is usually for a specific goal later on. Teddy may want to save for a new toy next month or he may want to have money saved to take on your vacation later this year. Or he may not. The words you use are secondary in importance; it's the decision-making process that counts.

> The parents (and kids) who seem the happiest and most financially successful are the ones who clearly distinguish between material luxuries and family necessities.
>
> – Eric Tyson[32]

Good Decision?
Bad Decision?
It Doesn't Matter

Here's a big growth moment: let your child settle on whether he wants to move some money from Save to Spend so he can get that basketball sooner. Let him be fully in charge of that decision. It does not matter which choice he makes. What does matter is that he now knows he can make some decisions and be responsible for them. Whatever he chooses, Teddy will have learned a powerful lesson about how to use his resources. He'll be stronger and smarter.

Over the years as he keeps making "divide my money" choices, Teddy may regret some decisions but he'll feel powerful about others.

Let him make and live with those choices. Don't bail him out. When vacation time comes, if he hasn't saved enough for a big treat, mention that he chose last month to spend that money. Don't lecture. Don't cave in. Just remind him that he made a decision to use his money for something else and he will probably have to get something smaller on your trip. Show that you trust him to be responsible about his choices.

These are the truly teachable moments, especially as Ted begins to evaluate the wisdom of his selections. You may want to provide some advice but it's best if you offer yourself as a sounding board, not as an authority. There are only two things you should insist upon:

1. At least ten percent of the allowance (or job, birthday, or other money) be put into the Invest group.

2. Something be allotted to Share. Allow your child to find out what it means to choose between the four categories as long as those two conditions are met.

By the time he's in high school he will have developed more maturity and wisdom than most twenty-somethings in regard to money decisions.

▌ Make-Your-Own Bank Night

Now back to your evening of paper plate dividing: of course paper plates are only temporary places to keep piles of money. In a few days you and Teddy can make personal money containers.

You might gather together four boxes or jars. Cover them with wrapping or sticky paper or decorate them any way your child would like. You can even get creative and design dividers for one box (like an oatmeal container or a shoebox), punch holes in the top, and turn that one box into a perfectly divided 4-account bank. Put labels on and you're ready. You might talk about how to design your bank so the "Forever Fortune" account can't easily be opened. I have heard of parents who just buy four piggy banks and label each. That works too. (I hope you didn't smash piggy bank number one if you choose this idea!)

Whatever you do, your child will have a ready reminder that when we get some money we'll make some choices. Besides what we have to spend, we'll keep some to help others. And we'll save some for a long, long time.

It's natural.

▌ About the Giving Box

In 2011 the total of charitable contributions in the United States was 298.4 billion dollars. This amount covers only that which is tallied through IRS tax returns. Individual giving (to friends, neighbors, and family) makes the total much higher; nor is the value of time volunteered counted in this number. No other country comes close.[33]

Giving, helping, aiding others: it's all a part of our culture. Why?

Rather than condense the reasons into a few ideas, I want to share with you some comments I have read along the way. Giving has vast rewards for the giver, often even greater than for the receiver. Besides, it's often just the right thing to do. In his Nobel Prize acceptance speech, the great humanitarian Albert Schweitzer described his philosophy of life with these words:

> We must try to demonstrate the essential worth of life by doing all we can to alleviate suffering.[34]

We each seem to know this at some level. Even small children want to reach out and help a puppy who looks lost or a family whose home has been destroyed by fire. In 2005 a group of social psychologists conducted a study and found that "Spending on others, being charitable and philanthropic, boosts happiness."[35] Our own well being seems to be heightened when we reach out to help others.

Financial advisor Jean Chatsky explains:

> No matter how you give – and our research shows there's little difference in the effects of giving time, money, or stuff – the act of giving resonates in a positive way. Why? Because, it seems, giving makes you a happier person. [Givers] are more confident and more content. They're also happier with most aspects of their lives.[36]

In one global study, "the fact that someone had donated to charity in the past month was as much of a happiness boost as doubling household income!"[37]

If we encourage our children to give a little time, effort, or money to a good cause, does that mean we can help them grow as people? The answer is yes. Here's Jason Zweig in his book *Your Money and Your Brain*:

> Increasing your net worth is less important than maximizing your self worth.[38]

He suggests that there are three ways by which we find happiness:

Having   Brings short-lived happiness

Doing   Creates good memories that last

Being   Makes happiness a true part of our lives when we make a difference in other people's lives

> We translate into reality thoughts of poverty just as quickly as we do thoughts of riches. But when our attitude toward ourselves is big, and our attitude toward others is generous and merciful, we attract big and generous portions of success.
>
> – Napoleon Hill[40]

With all the emphasis through advertising on the "having" part of happiness, we as parents can rest assured that when we give our children a chance to do things and to be helpful to others we allow them to build a genuine feeling of contentment within.

David Bach, in his book *The Automatic Millionaire*, says "It is the flow of abundance that brings us more joy, more love, more wealth, and more meaning in our lives. The more you give, the more comes back to you."[39]

A child who continually gets something at the store each time he shops with Mom or Dad will eventually find less and less value in what he comes home with. But watch that same child at the holidays if he gets to pick a present for the community children's Christmas tree and spend some of his own money to buy it. The whole world changes: he has now opened his thoughts, his imagination, to the future joy of some other child, someone he doesn't even know. That experience can create a deep, powerful, lasting feeling of thoughtfulness and caring.

"The more you give of what is good and desirable – the more you get," say Napoleon Hill & W. Clement Stone, in *Success Through a Positive Mental Attitude*.[41]

Time and again, study after study, author after author assures us that when we share, we also receive. We receive gifts greater than those we have given because we receive the intangibles that make life fuller and richer. We give our time and we grow in understanding; we give money and we develop gratitude for our own circumstances in life; we give love and we reap appreciation, friendship, and fulfillment.

These are things that mere "saving" and "investing" cannot buy. So as we teach our children how to make sure they themselves will be financially secure, we can also teach them to be emotionally open and truly appreciative of all that is in their lives. That's the reason we include "share" in our children's awareness.

Here's a comment about her wise mother by Farnoosh Torabi in her book *Psych Yourself Rich*:

> My mom always said one of the keys to a satisfied life was not to keep your head in the skies but to be mindful of the less fortunate. … Having an awareness of what you have and what others have not keeps you grounded, appreciative, and respectful. It reminds you to embrace all that is good and positive in your life, your riches.[42]

Allowing a child the opportunity to decide how he or she wants to help make the world a bit better is a gift like no other. Again, it's the feeling of quiet ownership – ownership of decisions and of responsibility – that will allow your child to grow into an appreciative, caring adult. Here's more advice from Jean Chatsky:

> Teach your children how to give. Don't hide from them what you do to help others. Explain to your children why you help. Then let your kids give on their own. Make suggestions and offer alternatives, but let them decide. Chatsky offers one idea: for her birthday party your daughter might ask the other children to bring a donation to a charity your child has chosen.

When I was a middle school teacher I started a club called "Kids, Time and Money." One of the components of the club was that we give away some of the money we had earned, even while we were learning to invest. We would meet for hours to decide where our contributions would go.

Those meetings were inspiring: 12- and 13-year-olds passionately spoke for good causes and the group's decisions were always well thought out. The students often built a hands-on component into their giving, such as buying ingredients, preparing food, and serving it at our local soup kitchen. It was wholly obvious that the act of giving meant a great deal to these students, even as they learned about their own potential wealth.

Here's a final thought, one I find most powerful. It's a quote from Helen Howard in the book by Stephen Pimpare, *A People's History of Poverty in America*:

> Am I my brother's keeper? I have to be. We (the poor) know what the "nitty-gritty" poor is like. The "nitty-gritty" poor is the hopeless[ness] and bleakness we have to face night and day. You, the so-called middle class, and the rich, cannot begin to know how much harder we have to work, and still not accomplish a thing. … We try to make it, honestly we do; it's not a case of being "lazy" or not wanting things for ourselves, no matter what you have heard or what you may think. We do have dreams. We do have ambitions. Am I my brother's keeper? I have to be.[43]

Should My Child Get an Allowance?

Parents have differing ideas about allowances: are they good or bad? Do they encourage a feeling of responsibility or one of entitlement? If we want to give allowances, what's a good age to start? When should they end?

These questions are ones you and your spouse should discuss and agree upon. Allowances are neither intrinsically good, nor are they bad. It all depends upon your underlying thoughts. Here are a few suggestions.

First, I urge you to set the expectation that everyone can contribute to the well being of the family. There are plenty of jobs to be done. Parents work so they can pay for food and housing; children can clean up their toys and put their dirty clothes in the hamper. Everyone should pull his weight without expecting a reward for every little task.

My husband and I visited one family where the little one-year-old's job was to take his wet disposable diaper (well-wrapped, of course) out of his bedroom and throw it in the trash. Even little children have jobs they can do to help.

The big reward here comes from knowing we are all an important part of the family. We each add value to the group and personal satisfaction comes from that, no allowance required.

Money in the form of an allowance might be tied to a bigger picture. What about giving your children some money every month so that they can actually pay for some of the things they want? Instead of a reward for what they should be doing anyway, they might get a bit of money to budget. They'll use it if they choose to own something that is more about wanting than needing.

For example, it's fall and your child needs a new backpack for school. She might want to contribute to what you have set aside so she can get that really cool one instead of the basic backpack you have picked out. Or your middle schooler wants a great pair of shoes that you'd never buy. You might tell him you have $30 for shoes; now he can decide if he wants to use some of his allowance to add to that so he can get the pair he'd really like. Or he might want to save the money for something else.

This method can give your child the understanding that:

- He is important to the family.

- He is capable of completing important jobs.

- You know there are things he'd like to get that you can't always justify in your family budget.

- He'll get some money to save, spend, share and invest. He should always keep a certain amount to invest for his Forever Fortune, but he can make his own decisions about the other categories.

That's one take on the idea of an allowance, an idea that works best when your child is older, maybe around nine or ten.

What about younger children? Here's one idea, taken from Jeff Yeager's book, *The Cheapskate Next Door*. His friend Stacie Barnett set up a Candy-Land-type chart on her fridge. Her son could advance through the squares (each standing for a chore) as fast or as slowly as he wanted. The chores moved through three levels. When he accomplished each level he would get different rewards:

Level 1 Stacie would give one dollar to a charity of his choice.

Level 2 She would put two dollars in his savings.

Level 3 He would get three dollars to spend.

Stacie's son was seven years old and the plan worked well for him.[44]

Of course as your child grows up he or she will want more money to spend. The experience of a first job is a thrill. And it's a challenging, maturing adventure. Let the whole event develop when your child wants it to.

My older son described his first stab at getting a job as one of the scariest things he'd ever done. He stood outside the door of our local golf club manager's office, heart hammering, trying to get up the courage to knock and ask for work. He was nine years old. He got a job, biked to work daily, and advanced through the ranks every summer after that for years. What an experience that was, finding out he could be important to a golf course manager! Plus, he would soon have money of his own and now could plan which pair of skis to buy – he'd have plenty of money when winter came around.

> *As children get older and become indoctrinated into the world of shopping, all sorts of purchases come into play. Consider giving your kids a weekly allowance and letting them discover how to spend and manage it. And when they're old enough, having your kids get a part-time job can teach financial responsibility.*
>
> *– Eric Tyson[45]*

So, allowance or no? It's up to you. It should not be just an entitlement, but an allowance can be a big move toward self-esteem and independence.

That Savings Account at the Bank
What About It?

Your child is ten years old. She has developed a sense of the difference between saving and spending. She knows she can spend whatever she wants to out of her Spend box. She knows her Save box is there so she can set a goal and put money aside for it. She might be saving to buy family Christmas presents or to get a puppy or a new bike, but she can eventually spend all of the money in the save-for-a-goal category.

So what is this Invest money for? That's a fairly abstract concept but it's the one most important to her future.

You can explain to her that someday when she has more money you'll show her how to make it grow. Tell her that "invest" means to put money to use by purchasing something that offers potential profitable returns, and that you'll teach her how to do that.

Someday she'll be able to buy small pieces of big companies. Those companies make money, so she'll be able to earn something every time one of her companies does. Her Invest box will eventually earn a lot of money for her … when she's really old like you are now … and even when she's as old as Grandma and Grandpa. That's why you sometimes call it her "Forever Fortune" – it can grow forever if she does not spend it today.

This is when your child's savings account at the bank becomes important to her. Tell her that a few years ago you started a savings account just for her. It already has some money in it since you have put a bit in it every once in awhile.

Let her start putting her own money in the bank now. Every few months let her take her Invest coins to the bank, fill out a deposit slip, and get the experience of real hands-on depositing. Tell her she'll earn a little bit of money from this account since it's now in the bank, and when she has enough to buy slices of companies and earn far more you'll show her how to do that.

Now the word "Invest" becomes more concrete. This is another step that takes very little time. But it's time well spent. Your child now understands why she has kept a little bit of money in that Invest place. It's for her future. When she's really old. Like you.

Chapter Four:

Boy, Can That Kid Add!

The Top Ten Kid Money Mistakes:

1. Not separating wants from needs
2. Not saving, investing, and sharing
3. Restaurant eating (the "giant sucking machine")
4. Too much stuff: a feeling of entitlement
5. Using the Bank of Mom and Dad
6. Not learning about money
7. Being bailed out
8. Not talking about money
9. Not putting holidays in perspective
10. Not valuing money ✗ 46

Let's make sure our children avoid these pitfalls.
You've done a lot already if you have taken those
first steps from the last chapter.

What Have You Accomplished So Far?

- You have shown your small child that it's good to save a bit of money.

- By the time your child is in 2nd or 3rd grade you have taught him or her how to separate money into groups like:
  - Wants
  - Needs
  - Giving
  - Saving Forever

- You have allowed your child to make some personal money decisions.

- You have set up a minor's savings account that your child may not even know about yet.

No? You haven't had time to take this step yet? Please do it this week. Put $25 aside and start that account. You'll be amazed at how much better you will feel, just knowing that you can add $5 here, $10 there. You will be starting a move toward a great financial future for your child.

All this by the time your child is around eight years old!

Congratulations. You can bet your child knows something about finances already. Your coaching has not just been about money: you are also teaching self-respect, self-control, decision-making, the art of giving, and a host of other life skills. These lessons alone will keep your children off the Top Ten Mistakes List.

So where do you go from here? We'll discuss a few steps to take when your child is eight, ten, twelve, and in high school. Each age presents a good time to get to another level of financial maturity.

If your child is already way past these ages it's even more important to begin talking about finances together. Even if he or she is a young adult, read this chapter. You can discuss the ideas in a mature way. The timing suggested here is based upon earliest cognitive development and in no way excludes adults.

> Teaching your child how to make, spend, save, and invest money is more valuable than any money you could give them.
>
> – Daniel Solin[47]

When Your Child is Eight Years Old

You don't need to do much more for a few years after your child has divided his money into the groups we mentioned before:

Wants • Needs • Giving • Saving Forever

Good decision-making is one of the most important skills your child can develop at this age so don't take away that experience – or that pleasure. What may, in your opinion, be an unwise decision might provide your child with the best lesson of all. A mistake made young is usually a low-risk learning experience as long as you don't provide bailout money to repair that mistake.

Show your child that you think he can decide how to spend his "wants" and "needs" money. You may have to provide a bit of guidance, but he'll get better at it with each choice he makes.

As the years go by, don't budge on the Saving Forever or Giving accounts. To have something to share with others can open a child's heart. Let your child know that the Giving account might also include non-monetary actions. Money isn't needed in order to go over and weed an older neighbor's flower garden. But boy, does it feel good. And even though the Save Forever stash may be small right now, the concept is huge.

By the way, start using the word "accounts" if you aren't doing that already. That's what they are, in a sense, and your child will get used to thinking of his divisions as accounts like the ones he'll have later in life.

These lessons take minimal time. Don't belabor your points, just make your discussions natural. If you have come this far you can be sure your children are learning that money is a tool and that they can have some control over how to use it.

A Happy Tenth Birthday Present

Things are going along smoothly. About the age of ten you can give your son or daughter the key to a million dollar retirement.

In *Book One, A Powerful Force*, you read about four cousins who decided to save $100 each month until retirement. The fifth person, a little sister, decided she would do that also. Far outstripping her brother and cousins, this ten-year-old girl will have accumulated $1,189,133 by the time she quits work if she earns an average of eight percent in interest yearly. She will have invested a total of $66,000 over the years. That's a profit of well over a million dollars. It works, as you know, because of compounding earnings combined with a lot of time rather than a lot of money.

When your own child was somewhere around eight you probably showed her that she has a bank savings account and you let her start adding to it. Here are the next steps:

1. If it's large enough, tell your child that you are ready to move most of that money into an investment account, one that can grow faster. If there's not enough money you can work together to speed up the saving pace.

2. You can simply pick a mutual fund that is a "Target Retirement Fund." These are all-in-one accounts which, depending upon how many years are left until retirement, automatically allocate a certain percentage to different assets (for example, U.S. stocks, international stocks, bonds, real estate investment trusts, etc.). The allocations are adjusted as the owner gets closer to retirement so the money will stay safer. Most likely your child will be changing the funds as she matures but this is a simple and smart type of fund to use right now.

3. I have also mentioned index funds, which may meet her needs even better than a target date fund. The fees are low because there's no manager to pay and they typically perform as well as their benchmarks. Either type of fund would be a good place to start.

   You can invest in the fund of your choice through an online brokerage very easily. As I've said before, this saves a lot of money over the years because fees are lower than with personal advisors. However ...

THIS IS VERY IMPORTANT:

In the earlier chapters of this book you got some hints as to how to learn more about mutual funds. When you make decisions for your child, be sure to find out how the fund should be legally structured as well as in whose name the account should be held if you plan to apply later on for money for college loans, grants, etc. Your tax or investment advisor, lawyer, or a college financial aid person should be able to help you.

This is important: you don't want a scholarship or grant to be denied because you were smart enough to save and invest money wisely. Proper legal ownership of this fund could make a big difference in college funding, as well as in how and when your child can access the money. Spending the money to get solid advice will be well worth it.

▌ This One's Forever

This is one account that should never be touched. Start it. Add to it slowly or quickly. But never take money out: this is the beginning of your child's very own, personal, fortune. Life should go on as if it did not even exist (other than during the yearly check you'll want to do to make sure your chosen fund is still a good one.)

Keep a little money in your child's bank savings account. That will be a place where she can safely put part of her birthday or job money, holding true to the understanding that she should always save a part of her income. That money can continue to move toward her mutual fund account in increments of $25 to $50 or more.

Finally, this might be a good time to teach your child the Lesson of Our Quiet Fortune, which you first saw in Chapter Three:

**Of all the money we make, some should be ours to keep.
It will grow quietly for the rest of our lives.**

A Little Later

After you have Started the
Quiet Fortune Mutual Fund

Show your child in black and white why you started the fund. Tell her to pretend for a minute that she is your age (horrors!) Without a fund like this she might join the millions of Americans who have no money saved by the time she's as old as you are (double horrors!)

Now go to a simple savings calculator like Bankrate.com on the web. Plug in the numbers:

- Amount the fund starts with this year.

- An approximate amount that can reasonably be added each year. Play around with that. Start by adding "0" yearly, and then try $1,000, then $2,000 per year.

- A yield of 7% to 8%, compounded monthly.

- How many years until she is your age.

- Hit "Total" *(much better than having no money saved, isn't it?)*

Good enough? Not quite. Now do the same calculation but use Grandma or Grandpa's age. The difference could be staggering.

Let her know that this is why you have started her very own mutual fund today. It's a gift well worth giving – and a gift worth understanding.

▮ Twelve: A Great Age to Be

There is no group more magical than 12-year-olds. Unless, that is, it's 13-year-olds. One minute they are mature and thoughtful, the next they are reduced to tears by a look. They are delightfully funny, heartbreakingly sweet, demanding, endearing, whining, sneering, and huggable all within a ten-minute period. If you have a middle schooler you know this already. If you don't, get ready – you're in for a ride.

> ### Don't scrutinize or criticize. Keep it fun and be done.
>
> – Terrie Drake

You can make it a great ride if you have established a solid relationship already. That means keeping a parental eye on things while being willing to talk to your child on an adult level much of the time. All of that is a subject for an entirely different kind of book, of course. It's important here because by the age of 12 or 13 your child is establishing some important thoughts about life and the choices he will be making. Money choices are among those.

In her book *Not Much Just Chillin': the Hidden Lives of Middle Schoolers*, Linda Perlstein makes important observations about our pre-teens:

- Middle schoolers are "growing up faster than ever, their workloads piling on as quickly as their distractions."[48]

- "In the middle-teen years, social scientists have found, kids choose their mates based on more individual preferences, but at [12 or so] it's because the guy [or girl] is someone their friends would approve of."[49]

What does this mean in relation to helping our children become wise about money decisions? It means our teaching moments will probably not have a lot to do with money; there are more pressing issues. What friends think is often more important than what parents think.

Basically, we might want to stay away from too much discussion about being financially responsible, at least during the times when logic doesn't seem to be fitting into the picture. We can keep firm to the rule that our child must save a portion of his or her income but lectures will probably be inappropriate.

We need to understand that it's not considered cool for a pre-teen to be too logical or too smart. Sad as that may be, groups of middle schoolers can make life tough on each other if they don't fit in.

Your child will be forced to make many choices during this time; for example, whether to join or avoid the groups that form around experimentation with alcohol and drugs, dating, sex, heavy dependence on social media, etc. The pressure will be to "say yes" to those things and the going could get rough.

Money, other than having some pocket money or enough to buy the latest smart phone, is not high on the list of issues that confront our children at this age. So we might want to keep our parenting to a minimum when it comes to lessons about future fortunes. It's time to help guide them through the forest of truly critical issues.

That said, here are a few steps we can take when we sense the time is right:

If your child wants some new "gotta-have-it" item that is fairly expensive you have a good opportunity of helping out. You might ask what he has in that savings account at the bank. If it's not enough you may be able to offer a real business incentive.

One grandmother offered to buy her grandson a new bike if he would split his profits from his paper delivery job with her. He could use the rest as he thought best. Not only did he get the bike he was wanting, but this was the beginning of his realization that he could use his own talents and efforts, combined with other people's seed money, to make some good things happen.

By the way, this step of having had a job or starting a small business around this age is one of the most common and most influential experiences that multi-millionaire business owners talk about, even 20 to 30 years later. You can read more about this in Thomas J. Stanley's *The Millionaire Mind* and William D. Danko and Stanley's *The Millionaire Next Door*. Warren Buffett discusses this idea too. Check out his Secret Millionaire's Club on the web. It is designed just for this age.

Notice the word Buffett uses: *Secret* Millionaire's Club. Be aware that it might be best if your child is allowed to keep her mutual fund account a secret. Even though you started it for her you should let her keep her knowledge of it out of the range of other adults or kids. No one really needs to know about it. We're talking about personal security, not show-off time. Especially during school years, show-offs are shunned, and for good reason.

This is, however, the perfect age to have your child discover the potential of the Forever Fortune Fund. Here's a little story about the middle school club I started called "Kids, Time, and Money":

> In our club we sold snacks after school. We kept records of how much time each student worked and what our expenses were. A third of our profits went to charitable causes, a third to our school, and the final third was divided among the students themselves. Every semester the members got paychecks for their efforts. Yes, real paychecks. They were to save at least part of their income.

> But that was not the most significant thing we did. What always made the biggest impact was the day I taught our members how to figure out Compounding Interest and to estimate how their money would grow if they invested it over time.

I will teach this method to you here and I urge you to sit down with your middle school child to do the same thing.

I mentioned before that most of us understand that money can grow. We learn (sort of) about compounding interest. But most of us don't learn the most important parts of the lesson.

Today, generally speaking, schools are trying to teach financial literacy to more students. But the trouble is that they often have far too little time to spend on the truly significant ideas. If personal financial literacy is taught in school at all, teachers must often present dozens of concepts (from goal setting to job seeking to budgets to credit cards to buying cars to renting an apartment to … well, you get it) in a very short period. That's a lot to cover.

Even more important is the fact that, while a teacher might speak to a class about a financial concept, the really important part is follow-through. Your child's teacher can't go home with every kid to actually help start the saving process. In this lesson (as with so many others) it's the action that makes the biggest impression. You're not only the best teacher; you're also the follow-up and feedback. You're the one person who can make a real difference.

The most important thing is that your children realize we don't have to start out rich in order to become well off. We just have to start saving. Without that basic understanding, any other lessons they get in school about financial literacy will mean very little.

I said that middle school students do not want to be different from their peers. But a quiet evening when you allow them to visualize the future is well spent. I have seen young people light up a dozen times over when they realize that they personally possess the one most amazing advantage of wealth building: they, unlike almost everyone else, have Time. It doesn't take a lot of money if they have a lot of Time.

This lesson can be truly inspirational. It can secure in your child's mind the understanding that life can be about so much more than making money frantically: as long as financial security is taken care of steadily and slowly, your child won't be a captive of the earn/spend/worry process.

So sit down with your child some evening and tell her you'd like to show her something phenomenal. Tell her you're going to do this the long way just once, not with a computer. Because kids are so accustomed to getting answers in a split second via computers, you may meet with resistance. But do what you can (a small bribe might work, or dividing the session into two evenings). If it would make a difference, start with $1,000 on the chart rather than $100. Your child might be more impressed.

This lesson is all-important. The brain stores information far longer if it arrives through an action than if it comes through a couple of keystrokes.

> *Most Americans are not using these secrets (about how to get rich) because they are not taught in school the way they should be.*
>
> – Peter Sander[50]

The Best Money Lesson Ever

You'll need paper, pencil, and a basic calculator. At the top of the paper write:

Start with $100
Invest it for a long time.
Earn an average of 5% interest each year.

Make columns on the paper:

Year	$ to Start	x 5% Interest	Total (Start + Interest)
1			
2			
3			
etc.			

Have your child write $100 in year one. Now your child will multiply that 100 by .05 (5%) and write it in the next column. That amount is $5. He will have earned $5 in year one, so the total for the last column (the end of the year) is the starting amount added to the 5% he has made. This is year one:

Year	$ to Start	x 5% Interest	Total (Start + Interest)
1	100	x .05 = 5	100 + 5 = $105
2			
3			
etc.			

He will now transfer that $105 to year two because for the 2nd year he will start with $105, not $100, in the account. Then he will do the same calculation, but with more money:

Year	$ to Start	x 5% Interest	Total (Start + Interest)
1	100	x .05 = 5	100 + 5 = $105
2	105	x .05 = 5.25	105 + 5.25 = $110.25
3			
etc.			

It is important to make sure your child understands what he is doing here. If he has learned about percentages in school the concept should be clear. If not, go slowly and explain. Don't move past the first few steps until your child really gets it.

Once it's obvious that the concept is understood you can fill out the rest of the chart faster. Stop occasionally to point out that your child started with just $100 and has added no more money of his own. That $5 in interest the first year is not much. Talk about it: about how compounding interest looks like almost nothing at first, but at the end of a lot of TIME, it's amazing how much it turns into. That's because his interest is now earning interest, then all of that is earning interest, and on and on for years.

Here's the table you'll make for 25 years of investing. Copy it if you want to. Or just fill out this page:

Year	$ to Start	x 5% Interest	Total (Start + Interest)
1	100	x .05 = 5	100 + 5 = $105
2	105	x .05 = 5.25	105 + 5.25 = $110.25
3		x .05 =	
4		x .05 =	
5		x .05 =	
6		x .05 =	
7		x .05 =	
8		x .05 =	
9		x .05 =	
10		x .05 =	
11		x .05 =	
12		x .05 =	
13		x .05 =	
14		x .05 =	
15		x .05 =	
16		x .05 =	
17		x .05 =	
18		x .05 =	
19		x .05 =	
20		x .05 =	
21		x .05 =	
22		x .05 =	
23		x .05 =	
24		x .05 =	
25		x .05 =	

This is what your 25-year chart will look like when it's filled out:

Year	$ to Start	x 5% Interest	Total (Start + Interest)
1	100	x .05 = 5	100 + 5 = $105
2	105	x .05 = 5.25	105 + 5.25 = $110.25
3	110.25	x .05 = 5.51	110.25 + 5.51 = $115.76
4	115.76	x .05 = 5.79	115.76 + 5.79 = $121.55
5	121.55	x .05 = 6.08	121.55 + 6.08 = $127.63
6	127.63	x .05 = 6.38	127.63 + 6.38 = $134
7	134	x .05 = 6.70	134 + 6.70 = $140.70
8	140.70	x .05 = 7.06	140.70 + 7.06 = $147.74
9	147.74	x .05 = 7.39	147.74 + 7.39 = $155.13
10	155.13	x .05 = 7.76	155.13 + 7.76 = $162.89
11	162.89	x .05 = 8.14	$171.03
12	171.03	8.55	$179.58
13	179.58	8.98	$188.56
14	188.56	9.43	$197.99
15	197.99	9.90	$207.89
16	207.89	10.39	$218.28
17	218.28	10.91	$229.19
18	229.19	11.46	$240.65
19	240.65	12.03	$252.68
20	252.68	12.63	$265.31
21	265.31	13.27	$278.58
22	278.58	13.93	$292.51
23	292.51	14.63	$307.14
24	307.14	15.36	$322.50
25	322.50	16.13	$338.63

As he does the calculations your child will realize that having money in an investment account could be a pretty decent idea.

He'll also probably say that a lot of this writing is getting repetitive. I was obviously feeling that way by year 11 so I stopped writing repetitious functions down.

You can cut out any steps that seem to be tedious as long as your child gets the concept, but not sooner: understanding is the most important step. For example, he really doesn't need to write the same number in both the last column of one year and the first column of the next year so he can just leave that last column blank.

Also, he can eliminate the middle column altogether by multiplying by 1.05. The "1" equals the beginning amount for the year and the interest is the ".05." Multiplying by 1.05 eliminates the need for the addition step. Make sure he understands that before you take this shortcut.

So he can truly see the magic of compounding interest combined with TIME, he should add another 25 years to the investment. Here's the chart you can copy or create:

Year	$ to Start	x 5% Interest	Total (Start + Interest)
26	338.63	16.93	$355.56
27			
28			
29			
30			
31			
32			
33			
34			
35			
36			
37			
38			
39			
40			
41			
42			
43			
44			
45			
46			
47			
48			
49			
50			

And here's the 26-50 year chart with totals filled in. I have stopped the unnecessary steps at different intervals. The chart gets fast and easy.

Year	$ to Start	x 5% Interest	Total (Start + Interest)
26	338.63	16.93	$355.56
27	355.56	17.78	$373.34
28	373.34	18.67	$392.01
29	392.01	19.60	$411.61
30	411.61	20.58	$432.19
31	432.19	21.61	$453.80
32	453.80	22.69	$476.49
33	476.49	23.82	$500.31
34	500.31	25.02	$525.33

I have quit filling in the last column:

35	525.33	26.27	
36	551.60	27.58	
37	579.18	28.96	
38	608.14	30.41	
38	638.55	31.93	
40	670.48	33.52	$704.00

Now I have started multiplying by 1.05 instead of doing the steps of starting amount multiplied by 5%, then having to add both amounts together. By doing this I'm only filling in one column per year. It's fast, but it's imperative that your child understand it. Otherwise, use the longer method.

41	704.00		
42	739.20		
43	776.16		
44	814.97		
45	855.72		
46	898.50		
47	943.43		
48	990.60		
49	1040.13		
50	1092.14		

The below graph demonstrates the growth of $100 investment with adding nothing more:

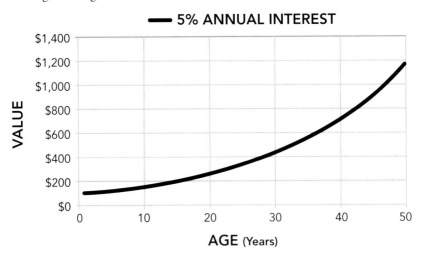

Now, Really: Why Do This the Long Way?

So far all of this has been about how to fill out a chart. I know it may look a little bit tedious at first. (Oh? Just a little bit?) You may be thinking of all the computer websites or spreadsheets out there that can show you in a split second the "value of $100 invested at five percent interest for 50 years." Why should we do this the long way? Isn't faster better?

No! Not for this lesson. I can assure you that "tedious" is actually superior in this case. You are teaching your child the single most important concept for his financial future, so do this as unhurriedly as possible, even if it takes several evenings. Completing the chart by hand and talking about it demonstrates how a mere five percent in interest can s-l-o-w-l-y turn $5 into $17 after 25 years, then $35-$37 in year 40.

Explain to your child that every single year he will earn the amount of interest shown on the chart and he'll be adding it to his last year's total. His money will grow and grow and he won't have to do another thing. Even while he's sleeping his $100 will be growing.

Plus, your child needs to see for himself (by doing the actual calculations by himself) that, at the end of 25 years, his $100 will now be worth $339. Does that mean it will be worth just double that in twice the number of years? No. With the power of compounding interest – actually the Miracle of Compounding Interest – his $100 is now worth over $1,000. That's almost three times more.

This is How We Remember Stuff!

It is important that your child manually calculate at least one chart of compounding interest if the many aspects of this all-important concept are going to stick forever. There will be plenty of other opportunities for your student to use websites, spreadsheets, and calculators for more revelations. For this one time, do it by hand.

Edgar Dale puts into statistics that which all teachers know:

We Remember:

- 10% of what we read
- 20% of what we hear
- 30% of what we see
- 50% of what we see and hear
- 70% of what we discuss with others
- 80% of what we personally experience
- 95% of what we teach others

Asking a computer to do a calculation fits into the ten percent or 30 percent categories, depending upon our personal involvement. Doing it with pencil and paper becomes a "personal experience" achievement with 80% recall. Your child will remember far, far more.

When you're finished this might be a good time to tell your child that he or she may easily get more than five percent return on a mutual fund over the years. Now you can go to a website under "personal finance calculators" or "savings calculators" to try out:

$100 invested @ 6%, 8%, or 10% for 25 and 50 years.

Here things get more exciting. Fifty years is a long, long time ("Heck, I'll be dead by then," you can hear your kids say.) But 25 years at eight percent doesn't look too bad. It's far more appealing to think about saving when you can see results like that, and far more understandable when your children know how the results came about.

Make the experience hands-on and concrete. You'll love to see those eyes light up, just like I did.

He who understands interest earns it.
He who doesn't understand it pays it.

Book Three
It's So E.A.S.Y.
For Young People

Chapter One:

A Real Fortune is Ahead

Mom and Dad,

Your kids are growing up fast and you've done most of the financial work so far. You've taught your children that saving is natural and that we should divide our resources into different piles. You've taught them something about compound interest. Maybe you have started accounts for your kids, maybe you were not able to.

Your children should read this book after you do. Young people are smart and they deserve to know the stuff that will help them in the future. What they learn – and what you discuss together – could skyrocket those futures.

To All You Students and Young Adults,

You can be wealthy. Most people aren't – you can be. It doesn't take much more effort to be rich than it takes to be poor. In fact, you can be kind of lazy about it if you want. But having money in your future is sure a lot more fun than having to worry all the time. Whether you strike out as an entrepreneur or work for a boss all your life, you can begin to take steps right now that will give you a better-than-good chance at accumulating wealth. These next three chapters tell you how.

It's actually simple to do.

What I'm going to tell you is something you might have heard about in one class or another. But there are so many things to pay attention to in school these days that it could easily get lost in all that other stuff.

This could be one of the most important lessons you ever get. It's the idea of how to turn a few dollars into the beginning of a fortune.

▌ To One Smart Kid: You

Someday when you're sitting in class, look around you. Probably 20-25 other people are in that room with you. Some of them are super smart, some not so. Some are rich or beautiful, some are exhausted, some worried. Some may seem like they already have it made while others may look like they've had no luck so far and don't know how to make things better.

You're somewhere in that mix. What you think of yourself today probably has something to do with comparisons. That's not necessarily such a good thing.

As soon as you get out of school those comparisons with classmates disappear. Flash! High school is over. Your life can now start in any direction you choose as long as you've learned some things along the way. Hopefully the direction you go will be one in which you get to do things that really, truly feel like you. Some day soon you'll get a chance to make choices that can steer you into a life you enjoy and have a great time living.

The future offers opportunities. Maybe you'll choose to stay in your hometown, maybe you'll move halfway around the globe. Wherever you go you'll find people, interests and groups that fit your personality.

It takes some thought when you make important decisions about your future, decisions such as: Will I like this? Does it interest me? Will it make a difference for others? For myself? That sort of thing. With some hard work and perseverance, you'll have options and chances to go where you want and do what you love.

So much for the philosophy. It's true, but it's not what this is about. There's one thing you'll really need to know, though, and that's how to get some financial security. Even if you plan to strike it rich someday you deserve the quiet knowledge that at some point in life you'll be doing okay enough to not have to worry about money.

Here's the story of Ana and Shawn, who could be a lot like you:

▎A Tale of Two Savers

Ana Gutierrez started saving when she was 22, right out of college. Saving involves an opportunity cost – the best alternative given up. It wasn't easy to save $2,000 a year then ($167 a month), considering her college loan, car, and rent payments. But Ana was determined to save because her grandmother always said it wasn't what you make but what you save that determines your wealth. So, reluctantly, Ana gave up buying that new car and renting a really nice apartment, and she saved $2,000 a year. She even told her parents she'd rather have a deposit in her investment account for a gift instead of "things." After 12 years, she got tired of the sacrifice, yearning for a brand new red sports car and other luxuries. She didn't touch the money she had already saved because she wanted to be sure she would have money for retirement, which was so far away that it almost seemed ridiculous to think about. She quit saving and hit the stores.

Shawn Wright didn't start saving until he was 34. He had also graduated from college at 22, but he had done without many things in college and, now that he had an income, he wanted some of those things. He bought a new car and a very nice wardrobe and took some wonderful trips. But spending his current income involved an opportunity cost. By the time he was 34, Shawn was married, had many responsibilities, and decided he'd better start saving and planning for his financial future. He had also heard that it isn't what you have earned, but what you have saved, that determines your wealth. He figured he had 25 to 30 productive years left in his career. So, with new determination, Shawn saved $167 a month (again, that's $2,000 a year) for the next 32 years until he retired at the end of his 65th year.

Which person do you believe had more savings at the end of their 65th year?

The Growth of Ana's and Shawn's Savings Charts

Age	Ana $ Added	Ana Total Value	Shawn $ Added	Shawn Total Value
22	2,000	$2,200.00	0	$0.00
23	2,000	$4,620.00	0	$0.00
24	2,000	$7,282.00	0	$0.00
25	2,000	$10,210.20	0	$0.00
26	2,000	$13,431.22	0	$0.00
27	2,000	$16,974.34	0	$0.00
28	2,000	$20,871.78	0	$0.00
29	2,000	$25,158.95	0	$0.00
30	2,000	$29,874.85	0	$0.00
31	2,000	$35,062.33	0	$0.00
32	2,000	$40,768.57	0	$0.00
33	2,000	$47,045.42	0	$0.00
34	0	$51,749.97	2,000	$2,200.00
35	0	$56,924.96	2,000	$4,620.00
36	0	$62,617.46	2,000	$7,282.00
37	0	$68,879.21	2,000	$10,210.20
38	0	$75,767.13	2,000	$13,431.22
39	0	$83,343.84	2,000	$16,974.34
40	0	$91,678.22	2,000	$20,871.78
41	0	$100,846.05	2,000	$25,158.95
42	0	$110,930.65	2,000	$29,874.85
43	0	$122,023.71	2,000	$35,062.33
44	0	$134,226.09	2,000	$40,768.57
45	0	$147,648.69	2,000	$47,045.42
46	0	$162,413.56	2,000	$53,949.97
47	0	$178,654.92	2,000	$61,544.96
48	0	$196,520.41	2,000	$69,899.46

49	0	$216,172.45	2,000	$79,089.41
50	0	$237,789.70	2,000	$89,198.35
51	0	$261,568.67	2,000	$100,318.18
52	0	$287,725.54	2,000	$112,550.00
53	0	$316,498.09	2,000	$126,005.00
54	0	$348,147.90	2,000	$140,805.50
55	0	$382,962.69	2,000	$157,086.05
56	0	$421,258.96	2,000	$174,994.65
57	0	$463,384.85	2,000	$194,694.12
58	0	$509,723.34	2,000	$216,363.53
59	0	$560,695.67	2,000	$240,199.88
60	0	$616,765.24	2,000	$266,419.87
61	0	$678,441.76	2,000	$295,261.86
62	0	$746,285.94	2,000	$326,988.05
63	0	$820,914.53	2,000	$361,886.85
64	0	$903,005.99	2,000	$400,275.53
65	0	$993,306.59	2,000	$442,503.09

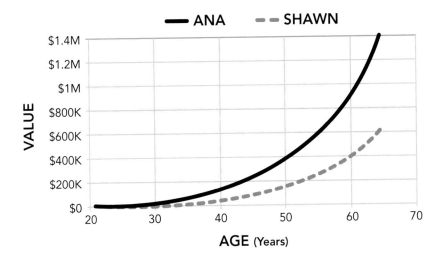

The Growth of Ana's and Shawn's Savings

Let's see what happened in the story:

- Ana saved money for 12 years.
  Shawn saved for 32 years.

- By age 65 Ana had invested: $24,000
  By 65 Shawn had invested: $64,000

- Ana's total wealth by age 65: $993,306
  Shawn's total wealth by age 65: $442,503

- Ana had put aside $40,000 less than Shawn but ended up with $550,803 more.

- By age 65 Ana's account was earning $90,300 each year.

Because she had started saving when she was young, Ana invested far less than Shawn, but she can now live on just her interest, keeping her principal intact to continue earning money. It's a win all the way around for her. If Shawn had only known about that bizarre little twist of compounding interest: it has to be started early.

Thanks to the Federal Reserve Bank of Philadelphia and the Delaware Council on Economic Education for granting permission to reprint "A Tale of Two Savers."[51]

▌The Guy With $42

Adam Shepard wrote a book called *Scratch Beginnings: Me, $25, and the Search for the American Dream.*[52] It's about the year Shepard decided to go out on his own and try to make it with only $25 in his pocket.

One of Adam's inspirations was a story he had read about a guy who went to a financial advisor with $42 when he was 28. "I don't know what to do with this money," he said. "But I want you to show me." He saved all of his extra money every month and invested it like his advisor told him to. Thirty years later he retired a millionaire.

From $42 to $1,000,000 in thirty years. Not bad. And not impossible. You're young enough to do the same thing. What do you need to do?

Save Some of Your Money

That's it. That's what you have to do. If you are already saving because your parents taught you how, then you'll quickly catch on to the idea that "Save" is, as one smart guy, Dr. Phil DeMuth, put it:

> The sum of all financial planning wisdom in one word.[53]

If you have that down you're probably one of the smartest kids in your class. You're instinctively on your way to financial independence. You're practically a paragon of wisdom when it comes to future wealth.

Here's another key word to add – invest. So there it is:

Save and Invest

Combined, these two actions become the single habit you need so you can accumulate resources for a financially worry free future. And you can do it practically no matter what you make: since you're young you can get it done.

Do Most Teens Save and Invest?

American teens earn billions of dollars every single year. That's billions – yep, nine zeroes behind it – a huge amount of money. It seems as though kids earning billions would be able to save some of that. But do they? No.

In fact, teenagers outspend what they make by at least five billion dollars each year – and their parents probably take up the slack.

These numbers come from Dr. Judith Briles who goes on to say:

> You can't help but wonder if a monster hasn't been created. What correlation can be expected between teens' spending and saving behaviors and those they display in adulthood, if they now outspend what they make by more than 5½ percent? The potential for indebtedness could be a financial back-breaker. It is, therefore, critical that [teens have] broadly based financial management skills.[54]

Let's look for a minute at why teens don't seem to be able to save money. DeMuth (the advisor who told us that "save" is the sum of all financial planning wisdom) also says this:

> Young people have thousands of uses impatiently waiting for their extra dollar: rent, clothes, car, drinks, restaurants, concerts, travel – everything. No wonder advertisers are so eager to recruit them.[55]

Check that last comment again. Advertisers set out to recruit you: they want your money! Please – if you get nothing more out of this chapter – know this:

- You have some money.
- Companies want to have it all.

- They don't think you're smart enough to save.

- They think you're easier to manipulate than most groups; they try every angle to make you feel like you won't be cool if you don't own this, play this, drive that.

- And they spend millions to get to your billions!

An onslaught of advertising is directed toward you. Here are facts from some experts:

- Outside of school teens are exposed to well over 3,000 ads every day.[56] With social media it's probably closer to 6,000.

- Many schools are also allowing companies to come into school in exchange for money.[57]

- Marketing to teens and young children is a serious business. Kids are told, rather directly, that they will be dorks or losers if they don't own particular products, and they are extremely sensitive to that kind of pressure, from little tiny kids to almost-grown teenagers.[58]

- The ads say, typically: "Buy me and you will overcome the anxieties I have just reminded you about," or "Buy me and be recognized as a cool person," or "Buy me and everything will be easier for you."[59]

- Teenagers are avid consumers and advertisers know their every statistic. For example, a few years ago there were almost 40 million teens in the U.S. Those teens went to stores and malls an average of 54 times per year, spending 1½ hours per visit, as opposed to adults who went 39 times a year and spent 1¼ hours each visit.[60] Look at that: companies actually calculate how many hours you spend shopping, and where you go. But they don't waste time on outdated statistics; they analyze your every purchase each and every day.

- Teens spend over $90 billion on food and drink each year and more on footwear and clothes.[61] Every bit of that spending is on record somewhere.

Advertisers know what you buy, how much you spend, and what can influence you.

Still not convinced that you're being examined and exploited? Here's a comment made by University of Illinois communications professor Robert McChesney on *Frontline* (PBS):

> Marketing companies hire people called "cool hunters." These people hang out online and in the teen culture to tell the companies what the latest trends will be – so they can "sell cool."

James Steyer adds:

> The whole point of marketers' relationship with teens is to turn them upside down and shake all the money out of their pockets.[62]

How are advertisers getting to our money? Here's Shira Boss in *Green with Envy*:

> The amount and pervasiveness of advertising increases constantly. The constant message is: You need this. You need this. You need this. You need this.[63]

By the time they reach the age of 65, most Americans are either dead broke – or dead!

– Anthony Robbins[64]

▌You're Smarter Than That

So should you shut yourself up like a hermit and never go out, never spend any money? Absolutely not. But I know you're smarter than to fall for those lines. Go and enjoy. But be sharper than those rich guys who are trying to convince you that life is all about image and buying stuff. When you get money, just keep some. Put it where you won't spend it. Know that it will set you up for a lifetime of "really cool."

Do just that one thing: keep some of your own money. You don't need to be as gullible as advertisers think you are.

By the way, think about a few little things that you pass by every day. Did you know that Americans spend about $30 billion every year on vending machines?[65]

Don't fall prey to those people who are getting rich by shoving things in front of you and taking your money. Think for a second and decide that you're on to their manipulations. You've got far, far better things to do than spend money just to make someone else rich. Especially when your money can – really and truly – make you wealthy instead.

It's easy. So easy, in fact, that you can just remember that word:

Earn
And
Save
Young

Here's one example of how easy it can be, starting with just ten dollars.

It's E.A.S.Y.
The Power of Ten Bucks

Let's say you're walking down the street looking in a store window and decide to go in. BIG SALE going on! You look around some, pull out three tees and think, "These are great! They're normally $21 each, but they're 30 percent off. I could get three for the price of two. And I need them."

So you get out your money or credit card and pay $42 plus tax instead of the original price of $63 and walk out feeling pretty good. At home you put them in your closet along with your other tees and decide you'll probably wear one tomorrow. Good enough. Right?

Well, right as far as this story goes. You have saved $7 on each shirt. So you saved a total of $21. And you will look good.

The math looks pretty good too:

Regular Price of Each Shirt:	$21
For 3 Shirts Normally:	**$63**
Sale Price of Each:	$14
For 3 Shirts on Sale:	**$42**

You've just saved the price of a whole shirt. Great!

… But you also spent $42. If you charged the shirts there's a good chance you (or your parents) will pay even more than the original price if that credit card is not paid off completely next month.

Here's where the power of ten bucks comes in.

Maybe instead of buying three, you decide you can make it okay with just two shirts. You put back the one you like least. You'll still look great but now you'll spend only $28 instead of $42. That's $14 less than you had first thought you'd spend. Walking to the cash register you glance at the little "paycheck card" (the one you're going to make and keep in your wallet) that says:

I earn $7.50 per hour:
2 hrs: $15
3 hrs: $22.50
4 hrs: $30
5 hrs: $37.50
6 hrs: $45 *(and so on)*

By getting just two shirts you will have spent $14 less than you might have. That's about two hours less you'll have to work to pay for your new clothes.

If you stop to consider what you just did you'll be aware that you made several good decisions:

- You found a sale.

- You needed (or wanted) a couple of tee shirts,

- But you really didn't need three.

- You knew how many hours of work that extra tee would have cost you, and

- You did not spend the extra $14.

But it gets better. Since this example is about the power of ten dollars, not fourteen, let's round that off, call it ten, and go on with the story:

You could just head home, happy with your new clothes. You could stop for something to eat; after all, you did just save money. Or you might not really think at all about what you spent or saved or the decisions you made.

But let's say that you actually do give a little thought to the money you just saved. Let's say that, on the way home, you decide not to stop for lunch or a snack to spend that "extra" money. If that happens you might just be on the way to real wealth someday. Why? Because $10 invested for a very long time can become a whole lot bigger. Here are a few "power of ten bucks" numbers:

Ten Dollars Invested:

# of Years	7% Return	8%	9%	10%
5	$14.80	$14.90	$15.66	$16.45
10	$20.10	$22.20	$24.51	$27.07
20	$40.39	$49.27	$60.09	$73.28
30	$81.16	$109.36	$147.31	$198.37
40	$163.11	$242.73	$361.10	$537.01

I know it may seem almost ridiculous to think about keeping the ten dollars you've just saved for as long as forty years. But that's what saving and investing are all about. That ten-dollar savings can become more than $500. If you save and invest it.

This is the very reason I'm writing to you today: doing things that seem as insignificant as saving ten dollars and investing it can actually make you a millionaire. You do not have to start out rich, you just have to start now to save some of your hard-earned money. Some of it should be for you, not for those advertisers.

Look back at that table for a second. Check how much faster money grows as more time passes ... and if you get a better average return. For a while it just goes along, goes along. But then it really speeds up until after thirty years your little tiny ten dollars has turned into $80, $109, $147, or even almost $200, depending on the interest it has been earning.

Now notice how much of a jump there is in the bottom column: it's that last 10 years that counts the most, not the first years. Time is important.

Here's the point: most people honestly do not think seriously about their futures until they are somewhere around 50 years old. Today millions of older adults are looking at almost empty bank accounts. In fact, one statistic says that the average amount people in their 60s have saved for retirement is $12,000. That's scary.[66]

Those people are really in trouble. Experts tell us that we should have over $1,000,000 saved (that's in today's dollars … think what that number will be when you're 60) before we retire if we hope to have a good after-work income. Almost half of our entire population doesn't have anything at all. Most of those people who are now near retirement weren't living in dire poverty all their lives: they could have saved, especially when we're talking about just ten dollars at a time. But they didn't.

You might think those people were just plain brainless. But there are lots of reasons for those numbers, some of which are beyond an individual's control. There was one concept, though, that could have kept them out of that situation: it's the knowledge of how sizeable a ten-dollar-bill could become if they had just decided early on to save and invest a few of them. By the time some people think about needing a bunch of money it's almost too late. Money is much harder to accumulate when it doesn't have time to grow.

I don't want that to happen to you. I want you to become financially secure. And you can. All you have to do is:

- Start saving some money now.

- Invest that money.

- Never take it out, even for that car you've always wanted (you have another account for that).

- Essentially ignore it except for occasional checks on its health.

If you do those things you could really, honestly have a fortune when you want to quit working.

If you think it's ridiculous for someone to be talking to a high school student about life years from now, I understand. It's hard enough to imagine even the day when you get out of high school or graduate from college or get your first "real job," much less think of the years when you're so old that you are ready to quit work. Your entire life is ahead of you: why should you even be reading this?

Well, I'll tell you. It's because plenty of experts predict that those statistics (like the one you just read about current 60-year-olds having only $12,000 saved) will be even worse in the future. The economy will probably tank several times, jobs are less secure, retirements are unpredictable, income inequality is growing rapidly, and you will most likely live longer. Oh, and advertisers are getting better at manipulating us.

Not to be too pessimistic about all this, but there's not much that's more difficult than being an old person who didn't have a clue that he or she should have been saving a little bit of money all along. And on the flip side, there's nothing better than having enough resources to pack up and go on an around-the-world trip if you want to because you were smart enough to stick some money in an investment years ago.

You can stay out of that poverty group of old people and join the travelers. You're young. You'll be just fine … if you take "Earn And Save Young" steps toward a great future. If you understand what this book is saying you'll be in a position to take care of yourself and call your own shots. You'll be so much smarter than those people who somehow just thought things would work out for them but who never even began to think about how they'd work out until it was much, much too late.

If those people could turn ten dollars into five hundred instantly, you can bet they would. That's one reason gambling and lotteries are so popular: people are absolutely desperate to make that magic happen overnight. But it almost never works out. Odds on lottery wins are millions to one.

You on the other hand, because you have time on your side, can make your money win over and over again. Use the EASY way.

What Should You Know To Build a Quiet Fortune?

You'll need a little bit of math, for one thing. A while back I told your parents that you are smart. But our schools have had a tough time compared with other countries, especially in science and math. That might be one of the reasons advertisers can grab so much of American teens' money.

Although math and reading scores are starting to rise[67] many studies back up the reality that our country is no longer as strong scholastically as it once was. Here's one fact: in 2012 the U.S. ranked 23rd in math among 66 top industrialized countries. Twenty-two countries, from Lichtenstein and Slovakia to the Netherlands and Singapore, beat us.

In his 2013 book, *The Price of Inequality*, Joseph Stiglitz argues that our lack of math background could be one of the reasons the rich get richer and the poor keep getting poorer. Maybe it's the way it's being taught, but many Americans find math intimidating or unnecessary. The fact remains, though, that "a knowledge of mathematics is the key to success in many areas of modern life."[68] There are at least a few concepts we ought to know about.

We'll take a quick look at those few math ideas. They can give us some thoughts about what our money can do.

Chapter Two:

Five Little Ideas That Can Make A Big Difference

Hundreds of books and thousands of articles have been written about how to get out of debt. Something really weird has happened in this American Dream country of ours if we need that much advice to convince us to correct our mistakes. Somewhere along the line too many people just forgot that we would get into trouble if we didn't know a couple of basic things about money.

Digging out of debt probably feels like cleaning an outhouse: you'd do almost anything to never be forced to do it. Let's keep you out of latrine duty.

Money Concept One
The Power of Compounding Interest

If you decide to save and invest some money, great! There's really just one thing to remember: time is one of the most important ingredients in the whole picture. If you don't know this, you could easily grow impatient and take your money out of your investment account to use for more "pressing" needs. That's because it doesn't look like you're getting rich until years have gone by. Growth is, indeed, very slow at first; it doesn't speed up until years down the line. But there comes a point in time that your money is growing so fast you almost can't stop it.

If you know how compounding interest works you'll keep investing.

For example: Invest $2,000 just once and keep it for 30 years
Earn 8% (compounded monthly)
and your $2,000 will become:
$21,871.46

Look at that – a little bit of magic has happened.

It will look like you've made almost no gain for the first ten years or so. But if you have $2,000 sitting around after your summer job, run – don't walk – to a mutual fund and shove that money in. Then forget about it (sort of) and never, ever touch it except to check occasionally that it's earning a decent profit.

About the time you're seriously deciding to quit full-time work and go do all those other things you'd like to accomplish, you'll have made $19,871.46. Do that every year and you'll have over a million dollars. Now, that you can enjoy.

In the first book of this series, *A Powerful Force*, I gave your parents a few examples of how a little amount of money can grow over time. Even though you may have heard about compound interest in school, go back to those stories and read them, especially the story about five cousins in Compound Interest Example Three. It could be the most important few minutes of your life.

No worries: I'll wait right here until you finish reading. Those pages just might change your life.

Really. I'll be here. The story's name is "Four – No, Make that Five – Cousins" and is found on page 19 of this *Complete Collection*. Find out how much richer Tommy becomes than Jane does, and on just $100 a month! Then check out what Tommy's younger sister will have if she invests in the story "Tommy's Younger Sister" on page 22.

Now I want to share another story with you that I also had your parents read. It's about Mark and Robbie, two friends from high school. It could be about you and your best friend. Go to page 30 to read "Two Good Buddies."

> **Almost one-third of American adults have a net worth of less than $10,000.**
>
> – Michael Milkin[69]

▍Apples to Apples

Okay. So far in this book you've read the "Tale of Two Savers" (Ana and Shawn). You have also read "Two Good Buddies" from *A Powerful Force* (Mark and Robbie). Three of those four people built something of a fortune. Let's talk about them together. If we want to see who actually did the best we should have numbers (percentages earned, years and amounts invested, and results) that are easy to compare.

In these stories Ana, Shawn, and Mark all saved $2,000 per year. Ana quit investing after 12 years. But she was still far ahead of Shawn because she had begun saving when she was 22 and Shawn started ten years later. It's obvious that investing early, even if you have to stop, will make an enormous difference (a $500,000 difference, in fact).

At first glance, Ana also ended up with more than Mark did, but that was because in "Two Good Buddies" Mark was getting a more realistic return of eight percent. If we compare apples to apples, bringing Mark's return up to Ana's ten percent, he would end up with $1,775,893 – very close to two million dollars.

So if we use a 10% return for everyone we see that:

Mark: Saves $2,000 yearly for 44 years (ages 18-62) ends up with $1,775,893.

Ana: Saves $2,000 yearly for 12 years (ages 22-33) then quits and ends up with $993,307.

Shawn: Does not save until he is 33, then saves $2,000 for 32 years and ends with $442,504.

To retire with any of these amounts is great compared with most people, but obviously Mark's method of $167 a month, which equals $2,000 per year, for a long time will bring the more astonishing results.

All three were better off than Robbie, though. He honestly will have a horrible time trying to find almost $2,000 every month to invest now that he's so much older.

> **Keep in mind that a part of what you have earned should remain yours forever.**

Why You Absolutely Need to Know This

More than half of Americans today will be living close to the poverty line after they quit working. And we're living longer. So their money could – and very easily might – run out. Done. No more left.

Walk along the street one of these days and look at people around you. Think about everyone walking past. You often can't tell who they are, but realize that less than half of the adults around you probably have enough resources to live well as they age. Imagine their worries, their constant fear that someday the piddlin' little bit they have set aside along with their small (and I do mean small) Social Security check will be all they have to live on. You can bet they wish they had started saving earlier.

But here's something: they probably never even knew how easy it would have been to accumulate genuine wealth. Now they're stuck.

The craziest thing about this (for you, it's the coolest thing) is that the younger you are the less you'll have to save and the easier it will be. That's why I'm writing to you, a young adult. Plenty of books have been written for people who are older and getting desperate. But you personally won't ever have to be reading those "How to save yourself even though you didn't do diddly when you should have" books.

Even a couple of years can make an enormous difference. Most people don't ever realize that.

How to Get Compound Interest Working for You Today

- Go online for tons of fun examples (because it's your fortune we're talking about here) of how money can grow for you. Just do a search for "Compound Interest" or "Time Value of Money" and play around.

- Look at the "Mom and Pop Plan" chart in *Book One: A Powerful Force*, page 48. Growth at the end is crazy.

- Get it into your subconscious that it may be tough to save something at first but you just need to start. Now. This week. Not next year or next month. Don't wait until you have $1,000. Start now.

- Are you too young or too broke to get $40 a week to save to get to that magical $2,000 a year? Start with five dollars, or ten; whatever you can. It's the habit of saving part of what you make that is the most important thing to do today.

- Do you get an allowance? Save some of it. Then invest it. The how-to of investing is in *Book Two: Learn, Invest, Teach*. Your parents have read it and you should too. Talk to them. Get a mutual fund. They'll help.

- Talk to your parents or grandparents about maybe not getting that (fill-in-the-blank) for your next birthday. Some money to invest would be great. It will be your seed money.

- Get a little job. It could be just a 2- or 3-hour-a-week job. Baby sit. Dog walk. Work at the local theater or restaurant. Mow lawns. Shovel snow. Teach swimming lessons.

- Get onto a couple of good websites. Although they change all the time, there are always thousands of sites that can help you look at your own possibilities. Two great ones are Bankrate.com and Mint.com.

- Don't fall for all those stupid "you need it now" messages. Remember that those advertisers just want to "turn [teens] upside down and shake the money out of their pockets."

- You don't need to feel any different from anyone in your class. No one needs to know you've made a smarter decision than anyone else.

- Better yet, share your plan and this book with friends. They, too, can get wealthy with this method.

- Keep reading. The next pages give you more ideas. Then after you've read them check out the other books. Know beyond the shadow of a doubt that, no matter what you earn in life, you can build a fortune.

Money Concept Two
How Important is a Measly One Percent?

One percent is really important. I'll tell you more on the next page, but here's a well-known little story about 1% of a dollar, or one penny:

One day a man offered his friend the choice to take either:

$30,000
or
One penny that doubles every day for a month.

The friend, excited about the prospect of getting $30,000 – picked the first option. Most of us (yes, they've even done studies on this "penny" story) would make the same choice. Unless we did the calculation first:

A penny that doubles in value every day would reach and pass the $30,000 mark by day 16. At the end of the 30-day month it would be worth over five million dollars ... $5,368,709.12, to be exact.

Now, this story is really about one percent of a dollar doubling (that is, growing in increments of 100% each time) not about having something grow in increments of one little tiny percent. But it's a fun thing to think about.

The one percent we're really talking about here is in percentage return on an investment. What's the difference between getting seven and eight percent over time, for example?

Let's look for a minute at $2,000 if we invest it for 20 years. We'll use a very simple compounding formula (only one time per year) so we can accurately see the difference that earning one percent more in interest can make.

After 20 years at these returns our $2,000 will become:

5% interest	$5,307
6%	$6,414
7%	$7,739
8%	$9,322
9%	$11,209
10%	$13,455

Every single percentage point increases the total by over a thousand dollars; the difference between earning seven and eight percent is $1,500. Now that's a big deal, especially if you have more than $2,000 invested. So as you look for returns, paying attention to a return difference of one or two percent is important.

By the way, when you decide to buy something by taking out a loan the same rule holds true. If you could get a loan on a car or a house for even a portion of a percent less through one lender you'll save a boatload of money, assuming everything else is equal. (Hint: Try a credit union when you look for a car loan. Their rates are usually lower than financing through a bank or dealership.)

▌Money Concept Three
▌How Do You Find Rates That are 1% Better?

Let's get one bit of reality straight here: very few investments in this world get a high return, say ten percent, year after year, without risk. At one point a few decades ago certificates of deposit earned 8% to 12%, and it was in real interest, not in the (somewhat) riskier stock market as earnings and dividends. Fast, ultra-safe growth just doesn't happen at this point in our economy. Everything goes up and down, from stocks to bonds to certificates of deposit, to real estate.

Even flowers go up and down. At one time back in the 1600s tulips in Holland began to sell at manic rates. Each tulip commanded an absolute fortune. Investors thought the value would continue to rise higher and that they could make a profit from the next buyer. Of course that didn't continue and "Tulipomania" eventually crashed, wiping out hundreds of people who had invested in the craze too late.[70]

Every investment swings back and forth. And the things that don't rise and fall will typically give you a low return because they're too safe.

What's an investor to do? I can't say this about everybody, but you personally have two very good ways to combat the uncertainty of an investment.

First, (of course) you have time. Right now you can take more risk to try to get higher returns. One way is to put your money into a "target retirement account" mutual fund. Those accounts put more of your dollars into stocks while you're still years away from needing your money, then very slowly make your investments safer (by buying more bonds and fewer stocks, for example) as you get older.

I know you'll be checking those investments as they get bigger, though, so you'll most likely be moving your money yourself rather than letting a target retirement fund control everything for 30 years. That way your percentages should be even better.

Another way to go is to find an index fund that has low fees. Vanguard and other fund families offer them. They just follow the stock market by holding the same stocks that are included in a certain benchmark, so they don't go through a lot of buying and selling. Investors (that's going to be you) don't have to pay high management fees.

Sure, the stock market will fall – you can count on that. But it has always earned big returns both before and after drops. And the average returns have always been higher than you would have gotten with super safe investments. You've got time to weather the bumps and get in on the gains.

Second, during times when interest rates are high you can find a place to put your money where it will grow more often than just once a year. Some investments, like certificates of deposit (CDs) or savings accounts, give you a predetermined percentage in return. Some will add those dividends to your total only one time a year. Others reinvest every quarter (three months) and others do that every month or even daily. Let's look at the difference compounding a different number of times per year makes:

We have $2,000
We are getting 6% interest
We'll keep it for 20 years

If it compounds: annually $6,414
                   quarterly $6,581
                   monthly $6,620

We didn't do anything personally, but because our money compounded more often with monthly computations we'll have an additional $200 from our investment. That's because the bank added in our interest 12 times a year so that extra interest was compounding also.

Now, frankly, a $200 difference after 20 years doesn't really thrill many people. So I'm going to give you a Never-Never Land example to make things more exciting. It's Never-Never because these days you'll be hard pressed to find any safe return as high as I'm pretending to make (ten percent). But once upon a time, back in the 1980s, CDs earned as much as 11 and 12 percent and even more. And they were completely safe. It can happen again.

Let's imagine that those days are back so we can really get the idea of compounding at different intervals. Remember, everything rises and falls. That goes for interest rates too. You may actually get ten percent on a CD or savings account some day.

You have: $25,000
You'll make 10% interest

Years	Annually	Quarterly	Monthly
5	$40,263	$40,965	$41,113
10	$64,844	$67,127	$67,676
15	$104,431	$109,995	$111,348
20	$168,187	$180,239	$183,202
25	$270,868	$295,343	$301,424
30	$436,235	$483,954	$495,935

There's a $60,000 difference in the 30-year row from Annual to Monthly compounding. Now that's a real improvement.

If you get a savings account, money market account or CD, try to find one that is compounded monthly or even more often. You'll find that information mentioned right after the percentage of return when you compare them online.

Money Concept Four
Sheltering Your Forever Fortune from Taxes

Now that you know how much difference one percent can make, imagine knowing how to keep most of your hard-earned money instead of losing it to taxes through the years. You can do this perfectly legally, and you should.

Mutual funds are excellent ways to accumulate money for all kinds of things. In fact, they are the most highly recommended way to invest, at least for "regular" people.

But there is a way to own a mutual fund so that it doesn't bring on too much of a tax burden for you. It's by setting your mutual fund up as an IRA, or an Individual Retirement Account; you can start one as soon as you begin earning money.

An Individual Retirement Account is really just for that: retirement. If you put money into a mutual fund and plan to use the fund for different purposes as time goes on, don't set it up as an IRA. If you will not use the money until you quit working, though, an IRA is for that portion of your earnings.

I told your parents in *Book Two: Learn, Invest, Teach* that there are several different kinds of IRAs. They each have different structures. Do a quick search and you'll find explanations online. For most young people, experts highly recommend Roth IRAs. Delaware Senator William V. Roth, Jr. sponsored the legislature to set them up in the late 1990s to help taxpayers in ways that Traditional IRAs did not.

Roth IRAs provide several advantages that had not been available before. For example, if you have never owned a house, you can pull money out of a Roth to make a down payment. If you do that with a Traditional IRA you will have to pay a penalty. In addition, taxes for Roths are set up so that you pay less in the long run.

While we're talking about retirement accounts, you need to know that 401(k)s are probably the best things you can become invested in if your employer offers them. Many companies offer matching funds if you contribute to a 401(k) through them.

Now we're back to that story of the penny doubling: if your employer matches your contributions put your money there. Everything you save (up to the amount the company will match) will be automatically doubled the second you put it in. What could be better than an automatic 100% return?

For more information about plain mutual funds as well as both of these "containers" to hold your long-term investments [401(k)s and IRAs] look back at *Book Two*, Chapter 1, "The Basics of Investing." You'll learn a lot.

If you are smart enough to want to earn more in interest, and if you plan to keep the money for a long time, make sure you set up the most advantageous plan for yourself. There is plenty of information out there so spend an hour and learn some stuff when you get some money together.

This won't take much time, honestly. Talk to your parents. Go online to Vanguard.com or another mutual fund company. Talk to a financial advisor. Do something today. Today, seriously … not next week. You'd be amazed how easily next week can turn into next year. We're talking about a few minutes on the Internet to start growing your future.

Time is, as the lawyers say, "of the essence."

Money Concept Five
The Rule of 72

There are only a few "sort-of-math-like" things you should know. We've already talked about the big ones:

- The magic of time and compounding interest

- The difference one percent can make

- How to find better rates of profit

- Sheltering your money from unnecessary taxes

The fifth and last one is fun. It's part of those weird math things that I could never imagine. ("Who figures this stuff out anyway," I often ask myself, "and how?")

Anyway, this little wonder is called The Rule of 72.

Let's say you have $2,000 and you'd like to double that. You think you can find an investment that will give you eight percent on average. You want to know how long it will take to turn your $2,000 into $4,000. So what do you do, guess? No! You take that goofy little magical, weird, almost-perfect number of 72 and divide it by your eight percent interest.

What do you get? Nine. That's the number of years it will take to double your money: nine years.

What good does it do to know the Rule of 72? Here's an explanation from the Student Guide to the NEFE (National Endowment for Financial Education) High School Financial Planning Program:[72]

The concept of compounding means that your money is making more money even while you sleep. One way to see how powerful this can be is called the Rule of 72.

Mathematicians say that you can see how long it will take you to double your money simply by dividing 72 by the interest rate. So let's say your grandparents give you $200 for your birthday and you want to use it to start saving for your own car. If you put the money into an account that earns six percent interest a year, how long will it take to grow to $400?

72 / 6% interest = 12 years

So in 12 years your money will have doubled to $400. But what if your dad tells you about an account where you could earn nine percent a year on your money?

72 / 9% interest = 8 years

Now you will have that $400 in only eight years. By earning just a little bit more interest, you reduce the time to double your money by four years. And this doesn't include any additional money that you may put into your account over time, which would speed up the process.

But what if eight years seems too long to wait and you want the $400 in four years instead? The Rule of 72 can also tell you the interest rate you need to earn to double your money in a certain amount of time. So for four years it would be:

72 / 4 years = 18% interest

With only four years to invest, your money will double if you can find an investment that earns 18 percent. Of course, that may be difficult to do as the stock market typically averages only about 8 percent a year over the long term. But you can certainly see how even a small difference in the interest rate you earn can make a big difference in how quickly your money compounds – earning you more money – over time.

This works only when interest and dividends are reinvested and it doesn't take taxes into consideration. But it's yet another way to see how a difference in one percent can make a big difference in how fast your money grows.

Wikipedia clarifies the rule by saying, "Although scientific calculators and spreadsheet programs have functions to find the accurate doubling time, the [rule is] useful for mental calculations and when only a basic calculator is available." The Wikipedia article explains in much more detail how this and other rules of compounding were derived. (It also gives a hint as to who those brilliant mathematicians were who came up with this.)

Here's a little Rule of 72 chart just to make it all simple:

Rate of Return	# of Years to Double Your $
1%	72
2%	36
4%	18
5%	14.4
6%	12
7%	10.2
8%	9
10%	7.2
12%	6
18%	4
24%	3

So There You Have It
Five Things You Need to Know

- The magic of time and compounding interest
- The difference one percent can make
- How to make a higher percentage in returns
- How to shelter your forever fortune money
- The Rule of 72

This investment stuff could actually be intricate: plenty of people spend their lives analyzing the theories of investing. If you want to do that, great: economics and finance can be intriguing. But you don't have to study those subjects in great depth in order to prosper.

You also don't have to be the CEO of a billion-dollar company. You could be a creative soul who rarely thinks about money. You could be a nurse or a caterer, a social worker or a dockworker. It doesn't matter. What does matter is that you save some of your money every single paycheck.

There are two things all those analysts agree upon:

1. We must start saving and investing as early as possible.

2. "How much the families choose to save" is the key to the difference between who has wealth and who does not.

A financial advisor can handle the details of investing if it makes you feel more comfortable. Affiliated advisors (like an Edward Jones representative) pull from the expertise of hundreds of other analysts in their company and can present options that are best for you. They will visit with you any time without charge and will help ensure that your investments are practical and appropriate. Their administrative fees are higher than with index funds, but you personally don't have to do all the research.

Independent and fee-only advisors give you advice about a wide range of options, including all the fund families, but you pay for them by the hour or in some other way.

Your parents can give you good advice. I think you should read the first chapter of *Book Two* yourself to get an idea about where to invest your money and how to start the process. In addition, you can look at websites and books about investing, of which there are thousands.

One straightforward book which is updated often and available in many libraries is *How to Invest $50 to $5,000: The Small Investor's Step-by-Step Plan for Low-Risk Investing in Today's Economy* by Nancy Dunnan. It's particularly good for beginning investors, with sections such as: "Safe Stashing for the First $50" and "The First $500."

Whatever you do next, save a little bit of the money that's in your wallet or your next paycheck or allowance. Make your start right now.

> *Begin earning and investing early in your adult life. Remember, wealth is blind. It cares not if its patrons are well educated.*
>
> – Stanley & Danko[74]

Chapter Three:

Beyond the Math – Jobs, College, Out on Your Own

You have the idea. It's E.A.S.Y. :

Earn
And
Save
Young

Ten dollars can turn into hundreds. You literally don't have to do anything except get some money then invest part of it. Every day from then on, and every night, even when you're sleeping, your money is working for you. It's earning a penny here, a dime there; and when you're ready to use some of your investment that ten dollars will have doubled and doubled and doubled again.

So, How Do You "Get" Money?

If you're old enough to save you're old enough to have a job. Don't know how to find one?

First, consider yourself lucky: because you don't have to support anyone else you can even create a job for yourself to earn just a little extra. You may find yourself on the road to entrepreneurship just by figuring out a way to earn money while you're young. Who knows?

Do you get an allowance? If so, make sure you actually earn it by doing jobs your parents need to have done. If they are paying you, you should deserve that money, not just because you're cute and cuddly, but because you're helping to make their lives easier.

If you are at least 14 you can start looking for a "real job" in restaurants, stores and other non-manufacturing, non-mining, and non-hazardous places. The list of possibilities is long and includes all sorts of things like being a bagger at a supermarket, an umpire or referee for kids' organized games, a camp counselor, car wash attendant, dishwasher or lifeguard. One of the best ways to generate ideas is to go online. Just search for "jobs for kids" or "jobs for teens" and the list of websites you'll get is at least 300,000,000 long (yes, that's 300 million).

Starting your first job can be scary and nerve-wracking. Within a few weeks, though, you'll look back at the younger you and smile. There are lots of rewards that can come your way besides a paycheck and you'll be proud of the confidence and self-esteem that appear along with the responsibility of your job.

In addition, each time you show up for work prepared, on time, and ready to do more than you're asked (that means you'll see something that needs to be done and not wait to be told to do it) you'll be developing skills that will make you a standout for other jobs, promotions, or recognition. Employers need problem-solvers, not problem-causers, and they will recognize you as being part of their solutions group.

And when you get that first paycheck, take out ten percent – a good amount to aim for – right away to put into your Quiet Fortune Fund.

> *Even if you have $50 there is a place for you to put it to invest and save. But there are different places for every kind of amount, so you can "branch out" as your savings grow.*
>
> –Nancy Dunnan[74]

Saving Some of this New Money

No matter what you are paid, decide that you're going to save something from your very first job. If your neighbor gives you five dollars for a week of dog walking, take at least fifty cents out before you go anywhere. Fifty cents is nothing, right? Why bother? Well, when you're dealing with any amount of money, realize that it's just what you do. Whether you earn five dollars or $5,000, you'll have the habit of putting ten percent aside before you do anything else. This truly is the only habit you'll need.

Way back in these books I gave your parents the Lesson of the Forever Fortune. Make it your financial mantra:

**Of all the money I make, some should be mine to keep.
It will grow quietly for the rest of my life.**

Make saving feel as natural as breathing: it's just what you do.

By next summer your neighbor might have paid you $250 and you will have stashed at least $25 of that. You might also have bought enough stuff with your earnings and now you're saving even more. Maybe you'll have put aside $100. Your savings habit has started.

No doubt you'll want to buy some special things with part of your hard earned money, and you'll deserve to. Just keep in mind that ten percent of what you have earned should remain yours forever. You don't have to be a miser – ever – if you just keep the power of saving going. (Nobody likes a miser, nobody.)

A Few Ideas to Help You Spend Less

Think about those advertisers who are out to get cash from you and your friends. Advertisers know most teens are easy targets and they're willing to spend plenty of time and money to analyze you. Be smarter than they give you credit for:

- Start using a waiting period of a few days before buying something big that you want but don't actually need. If you still want it later, fine. Chances are you won't want everything you first wished for. And you'll be glad you waited to think it over.[75]

- Remember the card in your wallet that converts your wages into hours? Add "minutes, days, and weeks" to the back. Then when you consider buying something figure out how much time you are spending at work to get it. If you don't want to pull out that card when you're out with your friends you'll still sort of have it in mind and the thought will help you make buying decisions. Whatever you choose you will at least have given it some consideration. That's the important thing.[76]

- Most millionaires know that "small expenses become big expenses over time." Figure out what those extra treats every day are costing you, then think again like those millionaires who also know that "small amounts invested periodically also become large investments over time."[77]

- Be aware of Opportunity Cost. That's the phrase economists give to the value of what is given up when you choose one option over another. If you choose to buy a new pair of shoes, for example, you might have to give up that night at a restaurant and the movies. That's not bad; it's just something to be aware of. Knowing about it is better than thinking you can "have it all," then going into credit card (or parental) debt. Or maybe you'll think of the opportunity cost of having to start college later if you decide to buy that car today. Being able to evaluate what you'll be giving up will help you make good decisions.

College: Will This Kill Your Investment Fund?

A lifetime of income inequality is clearly linked to education, especially higher education.[78] College grads earn an average of $800,000 more than high school graduates during their lifetimes. It's that simple: if you get some kind of degree beyond high school you are far more likely to make enough money to live well, share, save, and invest than if you don't.

These days in the U.S. we're seeing the phenomenon called "inequality" get rapidly worse. Basically, the wealthy are getting richer much faster than they ever did before. At the same time, people with lower incomes are quickly getting poorer. For example, young men ages 25-34 who have only graduated from high school have seen their real incomes decline by more than one-fourth in the last 25 years.[79]

Higher education is more important than it has ever been as laborers are driven out of jobs and their wages decrease. It is critical to you personally to get some kind of degree past high school.

You're also more likely to find a career that fulfills the heart and soul of you if you qualify for more jobs. Entry-level work can only keep a person happy for so long. So consider things carefully if you think an advanced degree of some kind is not for you.

If money is the biggest worry about college (isn't it for most families?) start right now to look for answers. Are you in high school and have a job? Set some of your wages apart for college in addition to the money you're investing for your Forever Fortune. Talk to your parents about costs: don't assume they have everything under control. On the other hand, don't assume there is no way they can help you get to college.

> *To meet the challenge of globalization and IT revolution and to achieve the steadily rising standard of living U.S. citizens have come to expect, Americans will have to Save More, Consume Less, Study Longer, and Work Harder than they have become accustomed to do in recent decades.*
>
> – Friedman & Mandelbaum[80]

Costs keep rising and may not be predictable, much less affordable. But there are things you can do. For example, look at Nancy Dunnan's book *How to Invest $50 to $5,000* for her section in the appendix called "Ten Steps Toward College Tuition." That section contains specific suggestions, phone numbers and web sites with concise, helpful information.

Take a few tricks from other people who have made it through. Some students seek a two-year degree from a community college, one that can transfer credits to a four-year university but that will cost just a fraction of what a four-year college will cost for those first years. One parent in a focus group offered to pay for school if her children were willing to live at home and go to a local college. If they wanted to go to another school the extra expenses would be theirs.

Grants, loans, and scholarships, of course, should be investigated with unceasing energy. Every hour you spend finding and applying for them could be worth hundreds of dollars. You don't have to be the smartest applicant to get financial help but you should be one of the most driven. Go to your high school library and counselors for all kinds of hints.

When you get into college you'll probably be living on scarce money. Think very carefully before you commit to a fraternity or sorority, a private or out-of-state school vs. a public institution, an apartment with expensive amenities, even eating at restaurants. Remember that almost all college students struggle financially so don't feel like you're the only one eating mac 'n cheese and rice 'n beans. It's better than thinking college means going out lots of nights to spend extra money from the Bank of Mom and Dad.

About Those Credit Card Offers

As much as you possibly can, avoid those tempting credit cards that are offered at every turn. The average college student these days graduates $29,000 in debt. Medical and other post-grad degrees can bring on ten times more debt than that.

As we all know (and as was corroborated by PBS News Hour on April 3, 2014) added credit card charges and interest can make college debt impossibly high. Dave Ramsey says the average college student gets one new credit card offer every few days.[81] There go those advertisers again, trying to turn your pockets inside out. Be as frugal as you possibly can and don't cave in unless it's almost a matter of life and death!

Here's an example of what credit card debt can turn into:

> Let's say you owe $10,000 on your credit card. Interest on it is 19.98 percent and you are able to pay only the minimum amount every month. How long would it take to pay that off? Thirty-seven years! You will have paid over $19,000 in interest alone.[82]

Far better to have gone out a whole lot less, to have paid with cash, sacrificed everything except your very existence, and come out with less debt. Besides, it's been shown that using credit cards can lead us to overspending by more than 20 percent. That's a lot, as you certainly know by now. In the DVD In *Debt We Trust: America Before the Bubble Burst*, Professor Robert Manning of the University of Rochester preaches against credit card debt for college students, as does expert after expert in every walk of life.[83]

> *With the over-abundance of credit available to people these days, many consumers have become much more childlike.*
>
> – Michael Schudson[84]

Be particularly careful if you are paying for things with your smart phone or another device. Every study ever conducted about how people get themselves into serious debt has concluded that we spend much more the easier it is to charge items.

So how can you avoid this kind of debt? Go lean, really skin-and-bones lean. Work. Yes, work one or more jobs at a time. It can be done. Take a lighter load and work another job if you have to. Find a financial counselor at your college and bug him or her with every single question you can think of. Go online for advice. Get names, numbers and web sites. Search hard. Find money, but try to avoid that nasty 20 percent interest rate of credit card companies. Shame on them.

College and Your Forever Fortune Money

It's during college and early marriage years that you simply may not be able to save much (if any) of your income. But I urge you to do a couple of things:

1. First, when college is over, try hard to get back to saving and investing as soon as possible. If you are still reeling economically, try to save two percent, then five, then seven. Within a few years you'll be up to investing a significant amount and again be on your way. Then no matter what you earn in your life your future fortune will be building.

2. Second, while you're in college, no matter what, do NOT touch what you already have in your investment account. Just don't touch it. Period. Ignore it for your entire college career if you can't add to it. Don't look at statements, don't inquire what it's earning, don't let yourself even think about it if there's any chance you'll consider withdrawing some.

When college is over you can come out of your cave and see how much you have. The temptation to use that money will have passed, I hope, and you'll be able to resume saving.

This advice will probably seem strange to you. After all, if you are about to go into debt for $2,000 and you have $4,000 in your investment account, doesn't it just make sense to use your own money instead of paying interest on a loan? At first glance it does. But coming next is another take on that situation.

What One Smart Man Said

I want to tell you about a much deeper, more meaningful reason to avoid digging into your investment account during college.

One self-made millionaire I talked to made an emphatic case for never touching savings. His financial success was due in part to his wise use of debt. He said:

> Keep saving, through thick and thin. (And things will get thin sometimes.) Even if you can only save one dollar, do it. That way you'll always have the thought that you're building your fortune, not that you'll always be poor. That mental thought – the knowledge that you'll be okay – is as important as having all the money you can possibly use. Save just one dollar. Then tell yourself things will be all right.

He also said this:

> If you have taken out a loan you know you have to pay it back. So you will. But if you borrow money from your own accounts you probably won't put it back. It's too easy to ignore, so you won't sacrifice as much. With a loan that has to be repaid you'll scrape together everything you can, get the loan paid off, and still retain the money that you had worked so hard to invest, the money that is already compounding.

If you take your own money out you could easily feel defeated and just give up on the idea of saving and investing. If you leave your personal money alone, though, you'll feel the opposite way. You'll know you had to go into debt to keep your life moving toward a goal. You'll pay it off as fast as possible and you'll still be on track. Meanwhile, the money you invested will continue working for you.

It feels good, really good.

Debt
Go Into or Stay Out Of?

Wait a minute: there seems to be a contradiction here. First I tell you to stay out of debt, and then I say go into debt. Clarification, please!

Okay, here's the main idea:

Stay as far away from credit card debt as you can. Those interest rates are usurious – in my opinion they should be illegal.

Look for legitimate help in every place you can. Again, a college financial advisor might be a good place to start. Find one you can relate to, then stick with that person through college. A personal relationship can help him or her to keep on the lookout for programs that fit your circumstances. Apply for everything – grants, loans, scholarships. Check out books from your library about how to write winning essays. It's usually the most "real" essays that grab a reader's attention, not necessarily the most perfect and formulaic. Spend hours and hours looking for help; those hours pay off.

Speaking of paying off, look for jobs where you can earn the most. They include tip-producing jobs like waitressing at higher-end restaurants and valet parking. Can't find a job like that? Create one that you can charge more than minimum wage for. You can clean one house each week for more than you'll make working at a fast food place. I know people who have put themselves through college by trimming trees, designing web sites, grooming dogs and painting houses. If you have a skill that people need you can charge a little less than the going rate for professionals and get plenty of work. Plus, those jobs can usually fit into your time schedule, not an employer's.

Freelance work is ramping up all over the world through websites. One beauty of that is scheduling, of course, as well as the fact that literally thousands of opportunities are out there if you have a skill that people need, whether it be web design or dog walking. In January of 2015 *The Economist* reported:

Perhaps the most striking of all the on-demand services is Amazon's Mechanical Turk, which allows customers to post any "human intelligence task," from flagging objectionable content on websites to composing text messages; workers on the site choose what to do according to task and price.[85]

Looking for a job that can fit your schedule? The world, literally, is yours.

There's no doubt: college costs can be daunting and you'll be watching every penny. But remember that most of your fellow students will be in a similar financial situation during this period. At some point you'll be able to look back and think of the "fun" of being totally broke and having to figure out how to live on nothing. It's okay; as long as you weren't severely malnourished or freezing to death in an unheated basement you'll probably come out relatively unharmed. And you will have learned many lessons along the way that had nothing to do with your academic degree.

When You're Out of College and On Your Own

Finally! The day has come when you're out of school and ready to start your life. You're on your own and free! ... And still broke, but that's okay right now. If you have the knowledge that $10 can someday become $500 you'll keep saving and investing. Your prosperity and your possibilities will be growing stronger every day.

So what about all those people who fall miserably into debt within a few years of leaving college? Why are they soon in financial troubles that they never saw coming?

All the experts have analyzed this question. Even though the Great Recession of 2008 was clearly responsible for a lot of people's predicaments, additional causes for our nation's massive wave of indebtedness existed decades before that. Some of them are:

> *Nothing's further from reality than Reality TV. Even HGTV can give you the impression that every young couple must have a beautiful kitchen. What every young couple really must have is a beautiful savings and investment plan. They'll never regret getting one of those.*
>
> *– Terrie Drake*

- Overspending in every category: housing, clothing, cars, even choosing private schools for nursery-age children.

- Overuse of credit cards. It doesn't take long before credit card debt absolutely takes over. Bankruptcy lawyers say the pattern is common and insidious: one month a family can balance things by shifting around payments on several cards, and the next month they realize that they're drowning in debt.

- An "I can have it all" mindset that began in childhood and was never discussed in terms of financial reality.

- A lack of understanding of the power of saving early and often.

- There are lots of other theories, even one that analyzes various countries' rates of saving and compares those rates to the language structure. For example, English verbs can push the future far, far away linguistically, while in Mandarin Chinese the past, present and future are all expressed with the same verb. That makes the future much closer in concept. Guess which country has savings rates as much as 25 percent higher? China, of course.[86]

The theories go on, and each one probably has some validity.

So many families are in financial trouble that an entire army of writers, advisors, and bankruptcy lawyers has sprung up. Look at the shelves on personal finance in any bookstore or library and you'll see dozens of books that cry out to us to Stop Spending! Get a Grip!

One financial author, Dave Ramsey, says, "If things are going to change, then you have to change."[87] He goes on to prescribe "Baby Steps" to get out of horrific debt and back to a normal existence. These steps are not complicated to understand but they involve such austerity and such a mind change that they are akin to a 12-step program to kick an addiction. They will take many years and a lot of severe personal discipline to accomplish, not to mention stress that can't really be measured.

Some people seem to think it's more important to be up to the minute on fashions and trends than it is to be smart with their resources. Those people quickly get caught up in a buy-it-on-credit trap that is excruciatingly difficult to break away from. If you may be heading down that path, congratulate yourself that you're reading this today. You know that you can make better money decisions now while you're young. You know you can end up better off than most people no matter what you make because of the things you do this very year, this very day.

▌ How Much Better for You!

Just think – you won't get into those dreadful situations that bedevil a lot of young adults because you already know the "sum of all financial advice":

Save

And you're doing it! Yes, college days are hard. Sure, you would love to splurge on that new car after you get out. But you have so much more: a future free from bankruptcy, overwhelming debt, and worry; a future that holds the promise of peace and security and growth. You'll have the same mindset that 60 millionaires expressed to Thomas J. Stanley, Ph.D., on page one of *The Millionaire Mind*:

> *Most people in bankruptcy simply don't see their debt building. They buy one thing on credit, then another and another. They keep juggling things until one month (literally, it's that fast) they realize they simply can't pay all their bills. No way to pay 'em all.*
>
> – Shira Boss[88]

> You cannot enjoy life if you are addicted to consumption and the use of credit.[89]

Notice the page number that last quote came from. It's the very first page of the book. In a hefty book – it's 406 pages long – this is the most important message of all from 60 millionaires that Stanley interviewed. You might be interested in reading *The Millionaire Mind*. It explores the way prosperous people go about building wealth, particularly those who started their own successful companies.

When you follow these millionaires' advice you will somehow adjust your lifestyle (smaller house? fewer new clothes? maybe keeping your second car for a few more years?) because part of your paycheck has already been given to the most important cause of all: your family, your future, and your children's security. It works.

Here's some very good news from Clark Howard on Evening Express: "More young employees are saving for retirement."[90] Vanguard and Fidelity, among other mutual fund companies, agree. This is most likely because Social Security and company retirement funds are visibly weaker than they were a decade ago and because it has become easier to invest online and automatically.

Too, during most recessions in the United States individual savings rates historically climb. People get shocked into saving because reality hits during those recessions. You can and should join the group of young people investing for the future. Then never stop. (Unfortunately, most people actually stop saving when times get better.)

Another good book among many that I'd suggest to you is *The Automatic Millionaire* by David Bach. He too teaches the value of saving a portion of your income and investing it. Bach uses the word "automatic" because automatically is by far the best way to save now that you have a real paycheck coming in. If some of your paycheck can go to an investment fund even before you see it, you'll always, always, always be on track.

Now, frankly, many families can't have deductions taken automatically from their paychecks when they are getting started: finances are just too tight and anything deducted automatically could catapult their bank statement into the negatives. But it is possible, until you get your footing, to be determined to hold onto some of your money even if it can't be the same amount every month.

I urge you to find some personal finance websites and books that look interesting. They contain many levels of advice, from the most fundamental to very detailed analyses of economics. Find what fits your area of interest and browse. But whatever they advise, each and every one of them is based on the thought that we should save something and invest it.

And you are on your way! Enjoy the trip!

> *Save as much as you can.*
> *Shelter every conceivable*
> *dollar from taxes.*
> *Invest prudently.*
>
> – Jean Chatzky[91]

Some Tips from "The Experts"

Linda, an officer at a local branch of a national bank, suggests:

Use your bank to set up several different savings accounts. You don't get much in interest but they don't cost anything to set up. Then you can have some dollars moved automatically into them each month for shorter-term goals. Set up accounts and call them:

- Car Fund

- Apartment Stuff

- Vacation

This works well for relatively short-term needs.

In unison, a focus group of 60-somethings all said the same thing when asked what was the most important piece of financial advice they would give to young people:

- Start Early!

- Start Saving NOW!

- From your first paycheck!

One of those focus group members added:

- Your retirement fund is untouchable. Never mess with it.

Another member added:

- You don't need everything you think you need.

Nancy Dunnan in *How to Invest $50 – $5,000* says:

> Please don't wait until your next raise, until next year, or until next anything. Waiting means never getting started.

Here's a bit of advice from a best-selling classic, *The Richest Man in Babylon*, by George S. Clason:

- Save just one dime out of every dollar you earn.

- Invest your savings, and the interest or dividend returns, from these savings and investments.

- Before you invest, seek expert advice on safe investments.

- If you need the money you are saving for living expenses or necessities, then work an extra hour (or more) so that you have no excuse for not saving ten percent of your earnings.

> *Always bear in mind that your own resolution to succeed is more important than any other.*
>
> *– Abraham Lincoln*[92]

Book Four
The VIPs:
Very Important
Parents & Grands

To All You
Very Important People,
Parents and Grands

"Your Choices Will Change the World."

That's a little slogan I keep propped up on my desk. The world? Well, maybe not the whole world. But our choices do certainly affect our own little corners of life, don't they? They also affect the lives of the people closest to us, no doubt about it.

I am writing this final book to you because you are some of the most important change-makers in the world. You are the parents, the grandparents, maybe the aunts, uncles or godparents of children and young adults.

We often say that young people are the ones who will lead the world into the future. But I think it's you who are steering behind the scenes because you have now spent a good part of your lives teaching them: the kids, the unschooled, the little ones. I know you've done your best because you love these young people more than life itself. You want them to be happy and to thrive.

Thank you. For getting this far in these books. For caring about every aspect of your children's lives, from their health to their peaceful wealth. You are their first teachers and their collaborators. Your choices have helped make your children who they are. And your job will not end.

Hopefully these pages will contain a few more ideas that you'll find useful.

> *Boomers can't roll back the clock, but they can certainly counsel their children. It's critical that boomers share their wisdom with future generations.*
>
> *– John Sweeney[93]*

▌ Personal Choices

As we adults look back at different personal choices we've made over the years there may be few we regret, but hopefully we're fairly well satisfied with our big decisions over time. Chances are the mistakes we've made came about in part because we didn't know all of our options or because we didn't know about the long-range benefits and repercussions of picking one option over another. To choose Door Number One over Door Number Three may change things imperceptibly at first, but the differences can grow rapidly and significantly as time goes on.

We've lived long enough to know which of our choices were good ones and which are regrettable. Of course we want our children and grandchildren to make fewer mistakes than we did (or at least different mistakes!) but they certainly don't want to hear just our lectures.

Kids do need guidance along the way, though. They have a forest of obstacles to navigate through as they grow up. Some kids get entangled or lost on their journey toward adulthood. If your children or grandkids are in that group – and by that I mean if they have gotten into drugs or other pools of quicksand – I urge you to do everything you possibly can to rip them away from those paths as fast as possible. Everything. That will be your first priority, the one that takes precedence over any other lesson you'd like to impart.

But young people are smart, intuitive, and curious, and if your kids are growing up with the normal set of issues that young people have, they would like to know something about how to handle their money. With only a little bit of talking you can give them information that they're not likely to get elsewhere but that could make enormous differences in their well-being later on. You are, after all, their most important teachers.

Where to Start
Or What are the Priorities?

These four short books have continually pointed to a serious problem and to a real solution. The problem, of course, is that far too many people face a frightening future when their incomes end. About the time we want or need to quit working, the large majority of us in the United States don't have enough to live on. At least half of us have almost nothing saved.

The solution, had it begun many years ago, would have been simple: start a habit of saving and continue it, moving those savings into investments. The largest part of this book has been about how to teach our children that concept.

But our priorities should always be our own well-being: becoming a burden to our adult children will do neither them nor us any good. If we are among the crowds that are worried about our finances we absolutely must look for answers to our own dilemmas. If we are close to retirement ourselves we'll need to hustle. On the other hand if we are young parents it's highly likely that we have not a penny to spare.

So what's the priority: the kids or us?

Have absolutely no doubt: you are the priority. Your own financial situation should take precedence. As we all know, the kids have time. We can find solutions to our own problems and we should be bent on getting on the right track as soon as possible. Putting any considerable amount of money aside for the youngsters will wait.

If you're young parents you may be starting both a family and a career at a low salary, or you may have begun a business and need to pour all your resources into that company's eventual success. If you're in that category, just knowing about time and compounding interest should be of value to you: it may help you as you try to make long-term decisions.

Older people may need to be reading, learning, getting advice, and maybe even finding another stream of income to beef up retirement savings. That's as it should be. Resources abound about how to avoid colliding with disaster if we don't yet have a significant amount of money built up.

It takes very little to turn the tide for our children, though. Even if we have almost no money to give our kids in the way of a "Mom and Pop Plan" account (see *Book One*), we can still give them knowledge, a sense of control, and good decision-making skills.

So if you have read these pages and at times thought to yourself, "Oh sure. As if we could come up with a mutual fund for our kids," please know that the starting-a-fund-plan is simply the "best case scenario" addendum to the most important piece: teaching your children how to save something of everything they earn. You can do that with only a couple of quarters lying around. You don't need thousands of dollars to teach with.

It's extremely important that you do teach something, though: as advertising, easy credit, and the culture of consumption continue to shape our society your children deserve to know something about how to take care of themselves. No matter who tries to part them from their earnings, our kids can and should learn to have power over poverty. It's a thing that needs to be taught. And what a teacher you can be.

> *How much the families choose to save is the key to the difference between who has wealth and who does not.*
>
> – Liz Weston[94]

One Simple Concept, One Simple Habit

Small habits begun early can help your children learn to make good financial decisions. Those habits are grounded in a simple concept:

Because of the power of compounding, even saving and investing a little bit can help us a great deal later in life, more than most of us can imagine. This is the most important concept your kids need to understand. Saving should be natural. This, as you know, is the one habit I keep talking about. Starting small and making it a way of life is a powerful way to go. Saving and Investing are choices that really can "Change Our Worlds."

You don't need to think your child absolutely has to start at an early age in order to assimilate these ideas. As with almost everything, "early is easy." But remember that overemphasis on anything can lead to obsession and your child should not be obsessed with money; that makes for a situation of miserliness, meanness, and even greed.

It's a life of financial peace your children deserve, and these little steps can help them develop that peace. Despite economic ups and downs they'll be able to live a life that can fulfill them, knowing that their choice to save and invest will be for their future financial security. Almost no matter what they earn they'll be okay.

Virtually all of the experts I have read – and I've read a lot – have agreed: It's not what we make that matters, it's what we save. I would add: It's also how early we begin to save that can make the difference.

▮ What Have We Covered?

Here's a look at what these books have talked about:

- Most important, the power of Compounding Interest combined with the power of Time.

- Simple ways to teach our young children how to save.

- How to help our children make their own money decisions since this is a low-risk time of life when they can make mistakes.

- How to teach them to divide their money into groups for different goals, giving them the knowledge that they really can control some things.

- How we (and later our children) can set up investment accounts even if we have not done that before.

- *Book Three* talked directly to our high school and college-age kids, especially reviewing math concepts that have to do with interest, and how they can use investments to build a quiet fortune.

What's still missing? Only a couple of points. The first is that, should you be able to set up an account for your children, that account should not be accessible to them without your knowledge and permission. There will be hundreds of times (literally) that the idea of having money sitting around will simply be too much for a young person to take: when they want a new car or a new house, when they fall into a trap and need to climb out, when, when, when …

Please seek advise from the fund manager, a tax advisor, or a lawyer as to how to set up any account so that you are in control. When you're sure the kids "get it" as to the importance of this account you can change things legally.

Just as important, you'll need good advice should your child be heading for college. Many grants, scholarships and loans take retirement funds into account as assets that the child has available to him or her. Those funds should not be included in the accounting of what your student actually can spend, so be sure the account is set up properly. Your child should not lose the chance to get financial aid simply because you both understand the value of sacrificing and saving early.

We have not covered an excellent way for you to save for college expenses. That's by using a 529 plan. For federal financial aid purposes, 529 plans are treated as assets of the parent rather than the child. This means your child has increased ability to receive financial aid when she has a certain amount in a custodial account in her own name.[95] You can learn about them almost anywhere. A good advisor will tell you how to set one up, either within his or her company or on your own.

What you know is important: what your kids learn is vital. You've taught them to save – now make sure they understand why they should.

If your child has not read these books (at least *Book Three: It's E.A.S.Y. for Young People*) you should recommend that he or she do that. Share the stories "Two Good Buddies" and "A Tale of Two Savers." They contain the key to how to become a millionaire without really thinking about it.

When you show your kids those stories the next step might be to help explain how hard (or easy) it will be to actually invest $167 each month. That's about $44 per week, or $2,000 a year, a good amount to aim for. Here's an inspired way to show your kids what that amount means in the big picture. Budget figures in a spreadsheet might work but they can't demonstrate the reality of putting money aside monthly.

What Big Income?

Dr. Judith Briles describes a truly in-your-face method she used to bring the real world of finance to her own children.[96] It's something you can do also. If you want, just use an average take-home salary for your profession. Here's what she did.

> Dr. Briles took her paycheck to the bank and cashed it. She asked for a variety of hundreds, fifties, etc., right down to ones and some coins.
>
> That evening she called her teen-age children to the kitchen table and told them she had just gotten paid and wanted them to see how much money she had. She dumped all of her money out.
>
> After their initial astonishment about how wealthy their mom was, Dr. Briles told them that she had to take expenses out, and they needed to help her figure out what would be left after paying her bills.
>
> So they started to remove money. First came rent bills, then utilities, then an average for food and so on. With each removal the pile became noticeably smaller.
>
> That evening Dr. Briles' children got a concrete look at what making a living really entailed and how much money was actually "her own" after all the expenses were taken care of.

That exercise was a brilliant one. It's extreme, and extreme experiences are usually unforgettable. I imagine her children thought twice from then on whenever they contemplated buying things before the necessities were paid for.

But there's an even bigger reward in store. It goes back to the Mark and Robbie story, "Two Good Buddies," that appears in *Book One*.

Mark put money each month into an investment account; it was definitely hard for the first years. Let your teenagers try to make that kind of savings happen during your family's kitchen-table night. First pull out that magical $167 monthly, which equals $2,000 per year, to save and invest. Not all that easy, most likely.

Next try to put aside the $1,560 per month that Robbie found out he'll need to save in order to catch up with Mark. Can it be done very easily with the money you've dumped on the table if you're also going to pay bills?

Whatever you can do to make an indelible impression on the kids, please do. The impact of your lesson could be, literally, awesome. You don't need to have started when your child was three, but it's a very good thing if he or she learns about saving at least by the age of 23. And you can teach those lessons without ever talking about your personal situation if you'd rather not.

> *Without knowledge of the disposable income of his or her family, or the efforts taken to acquire the income, the child has little sense of the barrier price provides against desire.*
>
> – Michael Schudson[97]

▌A Note for You Grandparents

You're important and you're loved. If you want to give your grandchildren a gift that is just as loving and important, here are a few ideas especially for you.

- You might want to set up a fund for each grandchild if you can. Consider:

  - A 529 to help Mom and Dad get a bit of college money tucked away. Check online or with a financial advisor.

  - A small savings account that could become the start of a mutual fund in a few years. I talk about this idea in the first book.

  - Consider setting up that "Mom and Pop Plan" mutual fund yourself if your own adult children can't do it right now but if you are in a position to. Of course, let the grandkids' Mom and Dad know what you'd like to do and why. They will probably be appreciative, but make sure.

- Perhaps some expert advice would be good. You might think of giving your grandchildren an appointment with a financial advisor as a graduation present. It could be one gift that keeps on giving for many years.

- Many successful people mention that their first experiences in the world of business came from their grandparents in the form of "seed money." One grandmother bought her 4-H grandson a goat that he raised and sold at the state fair. He paid her back with interest and invested his profits.

  In a less rural setting a grandfather bought lawn tools for his grandson on the condition that they share the profits from the lawn jobs he would do that summer. The list goes on and on, each young person crediting a grandparent with giving them a start and an incentive.

- If you want to give a straight-out gift of money, take the advice of dozens of advisors and make that money a true gift. If you offer a loan, be aware that family relationships can become strained if loan agreements are not strictly adhered to. Do be careful.

- Sometimes young people will listen to grandparents and hang onto their every word. If yours do, give them your thoughts about how to build wealth slowly but surely by saving and investing. In addition, be sure they know that you personally have lived through many down markets, but after each and every fall the stock market has risen even higher. When it's down your grandchildren's monthly investment will purchase more shares.

  The kids can also use your knowledge of how Social Security and defined benefit retirement programs have been severely depleted of late, making old age something we really have to think about. Young people often don't know about these trends that you have lived through or that this trend of a retirement crisis is fairly new, at least since the days when Social Security was young and healthy.

- Ask other people who are your age for the "one most important bit of financial advice" they would give a young person. Have them write that advice on cards if they are willing to, then show your "old-timers' advice" to the kids. You can share a good hour and a few good lessons.

- You might want to visit a bookstore and pick out a book about personal finances to give your grandchild upon high school or college graduation. One day I was at a large chain bookstore and counted no less than 75 different titles of personal finance books. Choose one that is geared toward inspiration or practical ideas; just letting your grandchild know you think his or her financial well-being is important says a lot. Or give them a copy of these books.

▌ Wisdom of Wealth

Grandma, Grandpa, Mom & Dad, and all of you who really matter to young people:

You have the ability to bestow the **Wisdom of Wealth** on those you love. You can give this gift in abundance and with love and caring, whether your own financial state is one of riches or of scarcity.

We are able to teach both the things we knew and what we might not have known when we ourselves were young.

And if we teach these lessons our loved ones will be wiser, their prosperity will be more assured, and their apprehensions about the future will decrease.

They will thank you for your practicality and your foresight.

I thank you also.

Of all the money we make,
some should be ours to keep.
It will grow quietly
for the rest of our lives.

Appendix

Investing Cheat Sheet
for Beginners

(Many thanks to Mindy White, who wrote a good part of this Investing Cheat Sheet for a college interest group about finances that she and I co-sponsored.)

- Debit Card
- Savings Account
- Certificate of Deposit
- Money Market Account
- Money Market Fund
- Individual Retirement Account
- Roth IRA
- Stock Market:
  - Shares
  - DRIPS
  - Mutual Funds
- ETFs
- Bonds
- Real Estate
- Other

DEBIT CARD
An electronic card issued by a bank that allows bank clients access to their account to withdraw cash or pay for goods and services. This removes the need for bank clients to go to the bank to remove cash from their account as they can now just go to an Automated Teller Machine (ATM) or pay electronically at merchant locations. This type of card, as a form of payment, also removes the need for checks as the debit card immediately transfers money from the client's account to the business account.

The major benefits to this type of card are convenience and security. Along with the convenience of accessing account funds at anytime it also removes the hassles associated with having to write checks as payment like showing ID and associated fees. Debit cards are also considered to be a safer form of payment as a code is required to access the account funds, while checks can be easily stolen.

SAVINGS ACCOUNT
A deposit account held at a bank or other financial institution that provides principal security and a modest interest rate. Depending on the specific type of savings account, the account holder may not be able to write checks from the account (without incurring extra fees or expenses) and the account is likely to have a limited number of free transfers/transactions.

Savings account funds are considered one of the most liquid investments outside of demand accounts and cash. ("Liquid" means that you can get to the money fast.) In contrast to savings accounts, checking accounts allow you to write checks and use electronic debit to access your funds inside the account. Savings accounts are generally for money that you don't intend to use for daily expenses. To open a savings account, simply go to your local bank with proper identification and ask to open an account.

Because savings accounts almost always pay lower interest rates than Treasury bills and certificates of deposit, they should not be used for long-term holding periods. Their main advantages are liquidity and superior rates compared to checking accounts. Most modern savings accounts offer access to funds through visits to a local branch, over the Internet and through ATMs.

CD (Certificate of Deposit)
A certificate entitling the bearer to receive interest. A CD bears a maturity date and a specified fixed interest rate, and can be issued in any denomination. CDs are generally issued by commercial banks and are insured by the FDIC. The term of a CD generally ranges from one month to five years.

A certificate of deposit is a promissory note issued by a bank. It is a time deposit that restricts holders from withdrawing funds on demand. Although it is still possible to withdraw the money, this action will often incur a penalty.

Let's say that you purchase a $10,000 CD with an interest rate of 5% compounded annually and a term of one year. At year's end, the CD will have grown to $10,500 ($10,000 * 1.05).[98]

MONEY MARKET ACCOUNT
An interest-bearing account that typically pays a higher interest rate than a savings account, and which provides the account holder with limited check-writing ability. A money market account thus offers the account holder benefits typical of both savings and checking accounts. This type of account is likely to require a higher balance than a savings account, and is FDIC insured.

Money market accounts are widely available and are offered by banks and other financial institutions. They are able to offer a higher interest rate by requiring a higher minimum balance, and by placing restrictions on the number of withdrawals the account holder may take over a given period of time. This restriction makes them less liquid than a checking account, but more liquid than bonds.

Similar to the interest earned on checking and savings accounts, the interest earned on a money market account is taxable. Account holders do not have to buy shares in a money market account, as interest earned on deposits is similar to interest earned on checking and savings accounts.

Banks issuing money market accounts take a low-risk approach when investing deposits.

Investors looking to purchase shares in a savings-like account can do so through a money market mutual fund, which typically has a share price of $1.

MONEY MARKET FUND
An investment whose objective is to earn interest for shareholders while maintaining a net asset value (NAV) of $1 per share. A money market fund's portfolio is comprised of short-term (less than one year) securities representing high-quality, liquid debt and monetary instruments. Investors can purchase shares of money market funds through mutual funds, brokerage firms and banks.

A money market fund's purpose is to provide investors with a safe place to invest easily accessible, cash-equivalent assets. It is a type of mutual fund characterized as a low-risk, low-return investment. Because money market funds have relatively low returns, investors such as those participating in employer-sponsored retirement plans might not want to use money market funds as a long-term investment option because they will not see the capital appreciation they require to meet their financial goals.

Unlike stocks, money market fund shares are always worth $1. What changes is the rate of interest those shares earn, called "yield." Some money market funds also come with limited check-writing privileges.

Aside from being low risk and highly liquid, money market funds may be attractive to investors because they have no loads (fees that some mutual funds charge for entering or exiting the fund). Some money market funds also provide investors with tax-advantaged gains by investing in municipal securities that are tax-exempt at the federal and/or state level. A money-market fund might also hold short-term U.S. Treasury securities (T-bills), certificates of deposit and corporate commercial paper.

A downside of money market funds is that they are not covered by federal deposit insurance.* Other investments with comparable returns, such as money market deposit accounts, online savings accounts and certificates of deposit, are covered. Money market funds, however, have historically been extremely safe investments and are regulated under the Investment Company Act of 1940.

*A note about this FDIC insurance: FDIC stands for Federal Deposit Insurance Corporation, which was started in the 1930s to protect against another Great Depression.

Ask if something is "FDIC Insured" when you open a bank account, savings account, CD, or money market account. Most are. That means you won't lose the money you actually invest. You may not make much money but you won't lose what you had.

Alternately, stocks and funds are not insured, but have a much greater chance of giving you greater rewards – sometimes extraordinary rewards.

IRA (Individual Retirement Account)

An investing tool used by individuals to earn and earmark funds for retirement savings. There are several types of IRAs: Traditional IRAs, Roth IRAs, SIMPLE IRAs , SEP IRAs, and MyRAs.

Traditional and Roth IRAs are established by individual taxpayers, who are allowed to contribute 100% of compensation (self-employment income for sole proprietors and partners) up to a set maximum dollar amount. Contributions to the Traditional IRA may be tax deductible depending on the taxpayer's income, tax filing status and coverage by an employer-sponsored retirement plan. Roth IRA contributions are not tax-deductible.

SEPs and SIMPLEs are retirement plans established by employers. Individual participant contributions are made to SEP IRAs and SIMPLE IRAs.

MyRAs have recently been established for those with lower incomes. Their initial investment threshold is lower than others.

With the exception of Roth IRAs, where eligible distributions are tax-free, eventual withdrawal from an IRA is taxed as income; including the capital gains. Because income is likely to be lower after retirement, the tax rate may be lower. Combined with potential tax savings at the time of contribution, IRAs can prove to be very valuable tax management tools for individuals. Also, depending on income, an individual may be able to fit into a lower tax bracket with tax-deductible contributions during his or her working years while still enjoying a low tax bracket during retirement.

ROTH IRA
Anyone with earned income can have a Roth IRA, even a child.
Under current law, qualified Roth IRA distributions aren't taxed,
no matter how much income is reported on the owner's tax return.
Unlike traditional IRAs, where distributions are taxed at
the prevailing rates, Roth distributions are not taxed at all (after age
59½, as long as the account has been open for more than five years).
The total value of the account will be the owner's to use, regardless of
how high tax rates might be in the future.

STOCK MARKET
What are stocks? Companies need money to operate and to
innovate. That means those companies use other people's money. The
people who loan them the money hope to make a profit in some way.
PARTNERSHIPS are a legal way to share ownership among a small
number of people, and there are other forms of shared ownership.

CORPORATIONS use STOCK. They divide ownership of the
company into thousands or even millions of equal parts, each of
which is called a SHARE. The people who buy those shares are
called SHAREHOLDERS. Even if you buy only one share you
are now a shareholder.

No, stock is not only for the already-rich. Some stocks can cost in
the hundreds or thousands but others cost $15 to $35 or so.

WAYS TO INVEST IN THE STOCK MARKET

1. **You can buy individual shares by going through a full-service broker** like Edward Jones, a nation-wide company with offices in almost every town. You always have an advisor to talk to but over time the cost of using a broker can be expensive and will cut possible profits.

2. **You can buy individual shares by going online** to places like TDAmeritrade and setting up your own accounts. Shares cost much less to buy and sell (maybe only $14 per trade), but you should know some things about what makes an investment a good one. Most beginners: trade too often, take bad advice about hot tips, buy when a stock has already gone up, bail out when the stock market falls, etc. Individual online investing is fun but it takes real knowledge and patience to make it work. Often a full-service broker can actually save you money by helping you avoid those expensive mistakes.

3. **DRIPS** are offered by over 2,000 good companies as a way to buy stock directly from the company (usually through a transfer agent) in very small amounts to large amounts, and usually on a monthly basis if desired. The plans also reinvest all or some of the dividends paid (it's up to the shareholder) into more stock; thus the name "Dividend Reinvestment Plan."

A Dividend is a changeable amount of money issued to their stockholders by some companies because they often end up with too much profit to be able to use it all. So they send the shareholders a small check…maybe a few cents to a few dollars per share…or they reinvest that for the shareholders in DRIPS.

Drips are a way to begin investing with a very small amount of money, and to keep investing monthly (or as frequently as you can afford) in small or large amounts, while reinvesting all dividends and avoiding brokerage commissions. In the long-term, it's a good and "patient" way to grow money over time, as you have dollar-cost averaging working for you as well, and you're investing, ideally, in great companies that you can't foresee selling at any time.

How to start? Look up http://www.fool.com/DRIPPort/HowToInvestDRIPs.html[99]

4. **MUTUAL FUNDS** were started at least 200 years ago because many people who weren't wealthy wanted to invest in the stock market but couldn't afford to do it. Companies formed to combine those people's money. Basically, the fund managers buy whatever stocks and other types of investments they think might be good, then they offer **shares of their mutual fund** to the public.

If you own mutual funds you may own pieces of several hundred different companies but you don't have to buy individual shares of each company; that would be cost prohibitive for many people. You will have to have an initial investment that may be relatively high (usually around $1,000) but then you can invest just $50 per month or so and keep your investments going.

When you buy an IRA, a 401(k) or a Roth IRA, you are essentially buying into a mutual fund that has tax savings built into it. They do have restrictions, however, about whether you can withdraw money from them without incurring significant tax penalties before you retire. Regular mutual funds don't have those particular tax penalties.

Anyone can invest in regular mutual funds. Warren Buffet recommends mutual funds for most investors as the best way to accumulate wealth. He goes further in recommending **INDEX FUNDS** rather than actively managed funds. Most experts agree with him.

Index funds are mutual funds that consist of the exact stocks that are in one of the many Indices (measuring tools used to assess the strength of different parts of the stock market). No administrator has to make daily decisions about what to buy, what to sell, how much to buy, etc.

If you buy an index fund you are trusting that the stock market will continue to rise over the years. You're not depending on one person (the fund manager) to be smart enough to make good decisions: you're depending on the fact that the stock market, despite a "correction" every 4 months – 4 years or so, will continue to rise as time goes on.

The cost to you of investing in an index fund is much lower than if you invest in an actively managed fund. An example: an index fund's cost could be .15% while an actively managed fund could be 3.45%. This makes an enormous difference over the course of years.

HOW TO START INVESTING IN MUTUAL FUNDS:

- Learn as much as you can. Start simply, with Wikipedia if you want to.

- Look at these three websites: Fidelity, Vanguard, T Rowe Price. They all sell funds with low fees attached to them. The websites have tons of information.

- Ask people questions. Call the companies. They are legally bound to give you correct answers. They are all easy to talk to: they want your business and will talk with you for an hour if you want.

- Save as much money as you can. Most funds require at least $1,000 to start. INDEX funds are most highly recommended by experts. Also, look at "Target Retirement Funds" as well as some others. (A few analysts advise us to stay away from target retirement date funds but many others say they are good vehicles, especially if you're not likely to pay a great deal of attention to your retirement investment.)

- Get a prospectus. READ IT. (Don't skip this step. You'll be a powerful, not a pitiful, investor.)

- Before you decide what fund to buy, look at the: 1-year, 3-year, 10-year, and "since inception" returns. Don't be fooled into thinking that a good 1-year average will continue.

- Call a representative and have them tell you how to enroll. You can do it online, but call them anyway; some of the forms look complicated but aren't. Representatives can simplify the process.

- Use Dollar-Cost Averaging. As soon as you can, make your investing automatic.

- Do not panic when the market goes down.

- The most important thing to do is start. You can switch to another fund within the same company at any time without a problem. If you later come across a fund that seems better, great. Just get some money put away today. You have an excellent chance of having plenty of money without having to suffer later on, but only if you start now.

- Stay interested in what is happening to your money. The U.S. and the world change quickly. You should look at your returns at least once a year. (Some people suggest doing this around your birthday.) You will make changes, even out of stocks and into bonds or safer investments. But you'll have been investing all along, and your money will be growing exponentially.

ETFs (Exchange-Traded Funds)

As you learn about mutual funds you'll hear a lot about ETFs. They have been available in the United States since 1993 and are a rapidly growing way to invest in the stock market. Basically, they are groups of bonds, stocks, or other investments just like mutual funds but they actually trade on the stock market. That means you can buy an ETF one day and sell it the next if you want to as the price goes up or down.

ETFs are becoming popular because they have several advantages over typical mutual funds. Among those advantages: they are liquid, structured for tax efficiency, and can be less costly than typical mutual funds to trade. This, of course, is a very broad statement because there is a wide variation among mutual funds themselves, and the same holds true for ETFs.

You'll want to learn about ETFs since they are quickly becoming a very popular way to invest. To learn more just look them up on the Internet. Also, check out web sites that sell them, such as Vanguard.com. As of this writing, Vanguard is the largest provider of mutual funds and the 2nd largest provider of ETFs in the world. It's a good place to start to get answers to frequently asked questions.

BONDS

Bonds are safe investments, but they don't have the same ability to climb that the stock market does. (They are usually low-risk, low-return investments.) Because they're safer most advisors recommend that all of us get more into bonds as we get older and closer to retirement.

You can buy a bond from a broker (those Edward Jones and Morgan Stanley-type companies). Usually bonds are sold in increments of $5,000. They pay interest and that interest comes to you 2 times a year in the form of cash. The rate of interest varies as the Federal Reserve Board meets and "determines prime interest rates."

What's a bond? A company (corporate bonds) or a government (municipal or government bonds) needs some money to pay for capital improvements such as streets, water projects, buildings, etc. They issue bonds, which are certificates like IOUs, promising to pay x% interest to anyone willing to invest in their building project.

Bonds come in different forms. Some are tax-exempt and are attractive to people with lots of income tax to pay; some are junk bonds, which pay more but have a default risk; some have great ratings of AAA and others are BBB investment-grade bonds. Confused?

Basically, talk to a financial advisor about bonds. The need for a person to invest somewhat heavily in them increases the closer one gets to retirement; bonds or some other safe investment should eventually become part of your portfolio.

REAL ESTATE
Real Estate is a completely different thing. If you physically buy a house or a piece of commercial property you usually need a lot of money for a down payment. Before the housing crisis in 2007 almost anyone could buy a house for virtually no down payment, but since then, it can be much more … as much as 30% of the value of the house or property in some cases. This varies considerably as economic conditions change and mortgage companies compete for business. You also have to pay a mortgage every month with interest. You will need to budget for regular upkeep, major repairs, and taxes.

In real estate investments some things work smoothly and others don't, but they are an investment that is far different from what most people take on. Investigate possibilities thoroughly; you're directly in charge of decisions, responsibilities, and eventual profits.

REITs (pronounced "REETS") are a way for people to get into real estate investments through mutual funds. The acronym stands for Real Estate Investment Trusts. You can find them in any company's list of mutual funds, usually with REIT in the name. They are a relatively new phenomenon and have been great some years and scary other years, depending on the demand for housing and commercial buildings.

OTHER STUFF

Plenty of other types of investment exist, many of which are obscure and risky to invest in unless you devote time to learning about them thoroughly. You can make a lot of money but you'd better be an expert, not a novice. They include things such as Options, Commodities, Hedge Funds, IPOs, and Foreign Assets (except those that are included in mutual funds; foreign assets in good mutual funds are usually an important part of your portfolio).

Works Cited

1. DeMuth, Phil. *The Affluent Investor: Financial Advice to Grow and Protect Your Wealth*. Hauppauge, NY: Barron's Educational Series, 2013. 13. Print.

2. Rhee, Nari. "The Retirement Savings Crisis: Is It Worse Than We Think?." United States: National Institute on Retirement Security, June 2013. Web. July 15, 2014. www.nirsonline.org.

3. Romans, Christine. *Smart Is the New Rich: If You Can't Afford It, Put It Down*. Hoboken, NJ: Wiley, 2010. 163. Print.

4. Rhee, Nari. "The Retirement Savings Crisis: Is It Worse Than We Think?." United States: National Institute on Retirement Security, June 2013. Web. July 15, 2014. www.nirsonline.org.

5. Rhee, Nari. "The Retirement Savings Crisis: Is It Worse Than We Think?." United States: National Institute on Retirement Security, June 2013. Web. July 15, 2014. www.nirsonline.org.

6. Olen, Helaine. "You Call This Retirement?" *AARP Magazine* Feb. 2014: 49. Print.

7. Rhee, Nari. "The Retirement Savings Crisis: Is It Worse Than We Think?." United States: National Institute on Retirement Security, June 2013. Web. July 15, 2014. www.nirsonline.org.

8. Rhee, Nari. "The Retirement Savings Crisis: Is It Worse Than We Think?." United States: National Institute on Retirement Security, June 2013. Web. July 15, 2014. www.nirsonline.org.

9. Olen, Helaine. "You Call This Retirement?" *AARP Magazine* Feb. 2014: 127. Print. (A quote from John Sweeney, Executive Vice President for Retirement and Investment Strategies, Fidelity Investments.)

10. Fullenkamp, Connel. "Understanding Investments." *The Great Courses*. Chantilly, VA: Teaching, 2012. 454. Print.

11. Reynolds, Susan, and Robert A. Bexton. *The 250 Personal Finance Questions for Single Mothers*. Avon, MA: Adams Business, 2009. 67. Print.

12. Bach, David. *The Automatic Millionaire: A Powerful One-step Plan to Live and Finish Rich*. New York, NY: Broadway, 2004. 36. Print.

13. Mandino, Og. *The Greatest Mystery in the World: Including a Precious Legacy for All of Us from the Old Ragpicker, Simon Potter*. New York, NY: Fawcett Columbine, 1997. 102-103. Print.

14. DeMuth, Phil. *The Affluent Investor: Financial Advice to Grow and Protect Your Wealth*. Hauppauge, NY: Barron's Educational Series, 2013. 19. Print.

15. Clason, George S. *The Richest Man in Babylon*. New York, NY: New American Library, 1955. 52. Print.

16. Fried, Carla et al. "101 Ways to Build Wealth." *Money* Volume 43 Number 4 May 2014. 53. Print.

17. Zweig, Jason. *Your Money and Your Brain: How the New Science of Neuroeconomics Can Help Make You Rich*. New York, NY: Simon & Schuster, 2007. 116. Print.

18. Fullenkamp, Connel. "Understanding Investments." *The Great Courses*. Chantilly, VA: Teaching, 2012. 185. Print.

19. Chatzky, Jean Sherman. *You Don't Have to Be Rich: Comfort, Happiness, and Financial Security on Your Own Terms*. New York: Portfolio, 2003. 109. Print.

20. Tergesen, Anne. "The Best Online Tools for Navigating Retirement." *Wall Street Journal* 20 Jan. 2015, Encore sec.: R2. Print.

21. Bissonnette, Zac. *How to Be Richer, Smarter, and Better-Looking than Your Parents*. New York: Portfolio/Penguin, 2012. 79. Print.

22. Maxey, Daisy. "When Is a Fee-Only Adviser Not Really a Fee-Only Adviser?" *Wall Street Journal* 11 Nov. 2013, Wealth Management sec.: R4. Print.

23. "The Top 40 Buffettisms." *Forbes*. 25 Sept. 2013. Web. 21 Jan. 2014. www.forbes.com/sites/agoodman/2013/09/05/the-top-40-buffettisms-inspiration-to-become-a-better-investor/.

24. Tergesen, Anne. "The Best Online Tools for Navigating Retirement." *Wall Street Journal* 20 Jan. 2015, Encore sec.: R1. Print.

25. Bissonnette, Zac. *How to Be Richer, Smarter, and Better-Looking than Your Parents*. New York: Portfolio/Penguin, 2012. 79. Print.

26. Hill, Napoleon. *How to Sell Your Way through Life*. Hoboken, NJ: John Wiley & Sons, 2010. 236. Print.

27. Rose, Charlie. Charlie Rose. PBS. January 19, 2011.

28. Olen, Helaine. "You Call This Retirement?" *AARP Magazine* Feb. 2014: 48. Print.

29. Tyson, Eric. *Personal Finance for Dummies*. 7th ed. Hoboken, NJ: John Wiley & Sons, 2012. 404. Print.

30. Schudson, Michael. *Advertising, the Uneasy Persuasion: Its Dubious Impact on American Society*. New York: Basic, 1986. 121. Print.

31. Solin, Daniel R. *The Smartest Money Book You'll Ever Read: Everything You Need to Know about Growing, Spending, and Enjoying Your Money*. New York, NY: Perigee Book, 2012. 186. Print.

32. Tyson, Eric. *Personal Finance for Dummies*. 7th ed. Hoboken, NJ: John Wiley & Sons, 2012. 410. Print.

33. Seefeldt, Kristin S., et al. *America's Poor and the Great Recession*. Bloomington, IN: Indiana University Press, 2013. 46. Print.

34. Schweitzer, Albert. *Albert Schweitzer: Reverence for Life; the Inspiring Words of a Great Humanitarian*. Kansas City, MO: Hallmark Cards, 1971. 24. (Excerpts from *Out of My Life and Thought* by Albert Schweitzer.) Print.

35. Torabi, Farnoosh. *Psych Yourself Rich: Get the Mindset and Discipline You Need to Build Your Financial Life*. Upper Saddle River, NJ: Pearson Education, Inc., publishing as FT Press, 2011. 27. Print.

36. Chatzky, Jean Sherman. *You Don't Have to Be Rich: Comfort, Happiness, and Financial Security on Your Own Terms*. New York: Portfolio, 2003. 165. Print.

37. Kitces, Michael E. "Happy Money and the Science of Spending – How Money Really Can (Sometimes) Buy Happiness." Kitces.com, 24 December 2014. Web. January 10, 2015. www.kitces.com.

38. Zweig, Jason. *Your Money and Your Brain: How the New Science of Neuroeconomics Can Help Make You Rich*. New York: Simon & Schuster, 2007. 265. Print.

39. Bach, David. *The Automatic Millionaire: A Powerful One-Step Plan to Live and Finish Rich*. New York: Broadway, 2004. 214. Print.

40. Hill, Napoleon, and W. Clement Stone. *Success through a Positive Mental Attitude*. Englewood Cliffs, NJ: Prentice-Hall, 1960. 9. Print.

41. Hill, Napoleon, and W. Clement Stone. *Success through a Positive Mental Attitude*. Englewood Cliffs, NJ: Prentice-Hall, 1960. 180. Print.

42. Torabi, Farnoosh. *Psych Yourself Rich: Get the Mindset and Discipline You Need to Build Your Financial Life*. Upper Saddle River, NJ: Pearson Education, Inc., publishing as FT Press, 2011. 27. Print.

43. Pimpare, Stephen. *A People's History of Poverty in America*. New York: The New Press, 2008. 40. Print.

44. Yeager, Jeff. *The Cheapskate Next Door: The Surprising Secrets of Americans Living Happily Below Their Means*. New York: Broadway, 2010. 92. Print.

45. Tyson, Eric. *Personal Finance for Dummies*. 7th ed. Hoboken, NJ: John Wiley & Sons, 2012. 410. Print.

46. Briles, Judith. "Money Smarts for Kids." Great West Great Teachers Financial Literacy Educators' Workshop. Denver, Colorado. 30 Apr. 2011. Address.

47. Solin, Daniel R. *The Smartest Money Book You'll Ever Read: Everything You Need to Know about Growing, Spending, and Enjoying Your Money*. New York: Perigee Book, 2012. 186-187. Print.

48. Perlstein, Linda. *Not Much, Just Chillin: The Hidden Lives of Middle Schoolers*. New York: Farrar, Straus and Giroux, 2003. 5. Print.

49. Perlstein, Linda. *Not Much, Just Chillin: The Hidden Lives of Middle Schoolers*. New York: Farrar, Straus and Giroux, 2003. 84. Print.

50. Sander, Peter J. *101 Things Everyone Should Know about Economics: A Down and Dirty Guide to Everything from Securities and Derivatives to Interest Rates and Hedge Funds– and What They Mean for You*. Avon, MA: Adams Business, 2009. 4. Print.

51. United States. Federal Reserve. Fed. Res. Bank of Philadelphia & Delaware Council on Economic Education. *Keys to Financial Success*. 2010. Print.

52. Shepard, Adam. *Scratch Beginnings: Me, $25, and the Search for the American Dream*. New York: Collins, 2008. Print.

53. DeMuth, Phil. *The Affluent Investor: Financial Advice to Grow and Protect Your Wealth*. Hauppauge, NY: Barron's Educational Series, 2013. 19. Print.

54. Briles, Judith. *Money $marts for Turbulent Times: Master Your Personal Finances in 30 Days!*. Aurora, CO: Mile High, 2009. 194. Print.

55. DeMuth, Phil. *The Affluent Investor: Financial Advice to Grow and Protect Your Wealth*. Hauppauge, NY: Barron's Educational Series, 2013. 19. Print.

56. Steyer, James P. *The Other Parent: The Inside Story of the Media's Effect on Our Children*. New York: Atria, 2002. 114. Print. (Note: Despite its age, or maybe because of it, this book presents a good history of television's changing roles in young people's lives.)

57. Steyer, James P. *The Other Parent: The Inside Story of the Media's Effect on Our Children*. New York: Atria, 2002. 114. Print.

58. Steyer, James P. *The Other Parent: The Inside Story of the Media's Effect on Our Children*. New York: Atria, 2002. 100. Print.

59. Schudson, Michael. *Advertising, the Uneasy Persuasion: Its Dubious Impact on American Society*. New York: Basic, 1986. 111. Print. (Note: this is an old book, but it was one of the first to accurately analyze what advertisers try to make us think about their products.)

60. Steyer, James P. *The Other Parent: The Inside Story of the Media's Effect on Our Children*. New York: Atria, 2002. 111. Print.

61. Steyer, James P. *The Other Parent: The Inside Story of the Media's Effect on Our Children*. New York: Atria, 2002. 115. Print.

62. Steyer, James P. *The Other Parent: The Inside Story of the Media's Effect on Our Children*. New York: Atria, 2002. 112. Print.

63. Boss, Shira. *Green with Envy: Why Keeping up with the Joneses Is Keeping Us in Debt*. New York: Warner Business, 2006. 71. Print.

64. Robbins, Anthony. *Awaken the Giant Within: How to Take Immediate Control of Your Mental, Emotional, Physical & Financial Destiny*. New York, NY: Summit, 1991. 27. Print.

65. Yeager, Jeff. *The Cheapskate Next Door: The Surprising Secrets of Americans Living Happily Below Their Means*. New York: Broadway, 2010. 53. Print.

66. Rhee, Nari. "The Retirement Savings Crisis: Is It Worse Than We Think?" United States. National Institute on Retirement Security, June 2013. Web. July 18, 2014. www.nirsonline.org.

67. Obama, Barack H. "State of the Union." State of the Union Speech 2015. U.S. Congress, Washington, D.C. 20 Jan. 2015. Address.

68. Stiglitz, Joseph E. *The Price of Inequality*. New York: W.W. Norton, 2013. 24. Print.

69. Milkin, Michael. "How Housing Policy Hurts the Middle Class." *Wall Street Journal* 6 March 2014. A17. Print.

70. Mackay, Charles. *Extraordinary Popular Delusions and the Madness of Crowds.* New York: Harmony, 1980. 89-97. Print. (Note: Originally published in 1841 under the title *Memoirs of Extraordinary Popular Delusions*)

71. Deaton, Dennis R. *Money, an Owner's Manual: A Personal Guide to Financial Freedom.* Mesa, AZ: TimeMax, 1991. 75. Print.

72. National Endowment for Financial Education. *Financial Education for a New Generation: Student Guide.* Greenwood Village, CO: NEFE, 2007. 32. Print.

73. Stanley, Thomas J., and William D. Danko. *The Millionaire Next Door: The Surprising Secrets of America's Wealthy.* Atlanta, GA: Longstreet, 1996. 75. Print.

74. Dunnan, Nancy. *How to Invest $50-$5,000: The Small Investor's Step-by-Step Plan for Low-Risk Investing in Today's Economy.* New York, NY: HarperPerennial, 2010. xi. Print.

75. Yeager, Jeff. *The Cheapskate Next Door: The Surprising Secrets of Americans Living Happily Below Their Means.* New York: Broadway, 2010. 33. Print.

76. Yeager, Jeff. *The Cheapskate Next Door: The Surprising Secrets of Americans Living Happily Below Their Means.* New York: Broadway, 2010. 23. Print.

77. Stanley, Thomas J., and William D. Danko. *The Millionaire Next Door: The Surprising Secrets of America's Wealthy.* Atlanta, GA: Longstreet, 1996. 54. Print.

78. *Inequality For All.* Anchor Bay Entertainment, n.d. DVD. Features conversations with Robert Reich, former U.S. Sec. of Labor.

79. Stiglitz, Joseph E. *The Price of Inequality.* New York: W.W. Norton, 2013. 8-9. Print.

80. Friedman, Thomas L., and Michael Mandelbaum. *That Used to Be Us: How America Fell Behind in the World It Invented and How We Can Come Back.* New York: Farrar, Straus and Giroux, 2011. 29. Print.

81. Ramsey, Dave. *The Money Answer Book: Quick Answers for Your Everyday Financial Questions.* Nashville, TN: Thomas Nelson, 2010. eBook. approx. p. 16. Web.

82. Bach, David. *Start Late, Finish Rich: A No-Fail Plan for Achieving Financial Freedom at Any Age.* New York: Broadway, 2006. 54. Print.

83. Schechter, Danny. "In Debt We Trust: America Before the Bubble Bursts." 2006. Documentary film.

84. Schudson, Michael. *Advertising, the Uneasy Persuasion: Its Dubious Impact on American Society.* New York: Basic, 1986. 121. Print.

85. "There's an App for That." *Economist* 3 Jan. 2015: 17-20. p. 18.

86. National Public Radio, aired 6 April 2014.

87. Ramsey, Dave. *The Money Answer Book: Quick Answers for Your Everyday Financial Questions.* Nashville, TN: Thomas Nelson, 2010. eBook. Introduction. Web.

88. Boss, Shira. *Green with Envy: Why Keeping up with the Joneses Is Keeping Us in Debt.* New York: Warner Business, 2006. 72. Print.

89. Stanley, Thomas J. *The Millionaire Mind.* Kansas City, MO: Andrews McMeel Pub., LLC, 2001. 1. Print.

90. Howard, Clark. *Evening Express.* HLN network, aired 25 September 2012.

91. Chatzky, Jean Sherman. *You Don't Have to Be Rich: Comfort, Happiness, and Financial Security on Your Own Terms.* New York: Portfolio, 2003. 109. Print.

92. Acord, David, and Abraham Lincoln. *What Would Lincoln Do? Lincoln's Most Inspired Solutions to Challenging Problems and Difficult Situations.* Naperville, IL: Source, 2009. Print.

93. Olen, Helaine. "You Call This Retirement?" *AARP Magazine* Feb. 2014: 49. Print (Comment by John Sweeney, Executive Vice President for Retirement and Investment Strategies, Fidelity Investments).

94. Weston, Liz Pulliam. *The 10 Commandments of Money: Survive and Thrive in the New Economy.* New York: Hudson Street, 2011. 44. Print.

95. Reynolds, Susan, and Robert A. Bexton. *The 250 Personal Finance Questions for Single Mothers.* Avon, MA: Adams Business, 2009. 98. Print.

96. Briles, Judith. "Money Smarts for Kids." Great West Great Teachers Financial Literacy Educators' Workshop. Denver, Colorado. 30 Apr. 2011. Address.

97. Schudson, Michael. *Advertising, the Uneasy Persuasion: Its Dubious Impact on American Society.* New York: Basic, 1986. 121. Print.

98. From Investopedia.com

99. Credit for this information: MotleyFool.com